A HOUSE
AT THE END OF
THE TRACK

A HOUSE AT THE END OF THE TRACK

Travels among the English in the
Ariège Pyrenees

MICHELLE LAWSON

Matador
9 Priory Business Park,
Wistow Road, Kibworth Beauchamp,
Leicestershire. LE8 0RX
Tel: 0116 279 2299
Email: books@troubador.co.uk
Web: www.troubador.co.uk/matador
Twitter: @matadorbooks

ISBN 978 1789016 901

British Library Cataloguing in Publication Data.
A catalogue record for this book is available from the British Library.

Typeset in 11pt Sabon MT by Troubador Publishing Ltd, Leicester, UK

Matador is an imprint of Troubador Publishing Ltd

This book is for everyone who has taken that step towards a new life abroad, whether by choice or through necessity.

CONTENTS

Prologue

LIFE IN FRANCE, IN ENGLISH

———

I stood at a crossroads in a small town in south-west France, trying to make sense of the directions I'd printed from Gerald's email. It was a Sunday morning in 2011, at that point between the seasons where summer was ready to tip over into autumn, but temperatures remained high and the town was dry and dusty as well as deserted. My eyes flickered around the two shuttered cafés and the browning verges but I couldn't see anyone to help unravel the directions. Turning left as instructed had inexplicably led me out of town, so I'd turned back and parked the car on the outskirts. In unfamiliar places I always felt more at ease on foot. I walked a few more steps and dialled Gerald's number, describing the arcade of shops opposite. 'I don't know where that is,' he pondered. I began to doubt whether I was even in the right town. I read out the crossroad signage and it seemed to click with him. 'Did I say turn left?' he mused. 'I wonder why I did that. You need to turn right.' We ended the call with a promise that he'd put the kettle on.

I was on a journey to join a dozen or so dots on a map of south-west France. The dots were English incomers who'd chosen to make a new life for themselves in the green foothills of the Pyrenees, more precisely the little-known département of the Ariège. Hardly anyone seemed to have heard of it, including a fair number of the English incomers before they'd moved there. In time I came to find that many had uprooted to a corner of France that they were unfamiliar with.

I'd become fascinated by the Brits in France and I was setting out to interrogate, and perhaps even violate, that English dream to move to France. I wanted to delve beneath the romantic accounts, the television programmes like *A Place in the Sun* and the property magazines that encourage people to sell up and leave Britain for a new life in France. I'd also become mesmerised by one particular Ariège-based website that was dedicated to *Life in France, in English*. There are internet forums all over France to help people plan their move and support each other, answering countless questions and so on, but this one was particularly lively, with members even arranging to meet up offline. I'd also noted a fair bit of sneering from certain members. Unhappily for some, the soap opera of *Life in France, in English* offered an easy platform for infighting, with a few old-timers condemning recent incomers who *have not done any homework; they do not know how to survive and they do not know anything about the country or language.* Personal rants railed against needy newcomers who were being *coddled, like cotton wool,* who could *not be bothered to get off their backside and explore a bit.* Vicious seething against migrants is nothing new, but here it was the Brits pitched against each other.

At one point I found myself logging on daily, drawn into it as if it were a television soap. My interest only waned as it became plagued by hundreds of spam memberships, triggering its eventual closure. Another member set up a replacement site in no time, which continues to support English-speaking incomers in the Ariège, noticeably minus the infighting that characterised the original *Life in France, in English* platform.

I'd begun to notice that British columnists based in France similarly had few good words to say about their compatriots. We're accustomed to seeing Britain's own immigration situation described in the tabloids using language such as *threatened, invasion* and *swamped*, but the incomers themselves were using it to draw a demarcation between their own behaviour and that of all the other *Brits in France*. That very phrase seemed to connote the negative side of things; I'd seen the title *Wake-up call for Brits in France* that introduced a story about the *harsh truths* of reality that contradict the initial dream of moving to France[1]. Telegraph writer Michael Wright observed that *all the Brits in France* seemed poverty-stricken – the *nouveaux pauvres* – who economised by buying items shipped over by fellow compatriots. It's hard not to smile at his description of the unloading of John Lewis pillows, fresh mushrooms and grated carrot from a British van.[2] Even a journalist of Belgian origin, Marc Roche, used the phrase to write about the limited adventurous spirit of the Brits in France who *listen to the BBC, make sausages and mash and drink too much wine.*[3]

The word *Brits* was often the word of choice when complaining, rather than *Britons* or *British*. People were quoted as having an *I didn't come to France to hang out with other Brits* attitude. The other Brits were the ones who had been suckered into buying *unsuitable properties,* and who'd come in such numbers that they found themselves in the ironic situation of having ended up with what they were fleeing – *other Brits*. And no surprises that it was used to refer to criminals in The Sun's story[4] about British cocaine smugglers

---

1   *Wake-up call for Brits in France*, Sunday Express, October 9 2005.
2   *C'est la folie,*The Telegraph, May 1 2010.
3   *Les Rosbifs du jour*, The Times, March 19 2004.
4   '*Soccer bungs cash used by drug gang': Shocking claims by Brits held in France,* The Sun, March 23 2010.

and the *raids on homes of more Brits in France's Dordogne region.*

Some writers saw it as an *invasion* of unprepared Brits who had come over because they'd *seen it on a television programme.* One particular article, by John Lichfield, warned readers to avoid the British hotspots such as *Dordogneshire* and *find a rustic retreat away from other Brits.*[5] Lichfield drew an unambiguous line between these recent *migrants* making up the *"new" British invasion,* and *the longer-established British residents.* Lichfield naturally included himself within the latter, claiming that the presence of the old-timer residents was *prized* by the local French for what they brought to the moribund villages. To be fair, there's a long tradition of anecdotes that justify the British incomers as active protectors of local heritage. There's been enthusiastic, as well as sometimes grudging, acceptance by the French that the British do a good job of restoring their decaying buildings. Besides, an influx of eager rural dwellers can bring life to dormant villages and help to revive local businesses. Despite a reputation for buying at inflated prices and driving up the average property prices, the French appreciate a British willingness to pay decent money for their old wrecks.

That's not to say that there's been no anti-English sentiment expressed by the French themselves in recent years. Following the large numbers of property seekers coming into Brittany, demonstrations in February 2005 saw protestors in Bourbriac claiming that Brittany "is not for sale". The French journalist José-Alain Fralon has written an entire book about the recent incomers in and around the Dordogne département: *Au secours, les Anglais nous envahissent!* (*Help, the English are invading us!*). Despite the tongue-in-cheek title and the invasion metaphors that repeatedly refer to the English as

---

5   *Find a rustic retreat away from other Brits.* The Independent, January 14 2004.

our best, our oldest, our most sincere enemies, the examples that he gives of French resentment seem underwhelming. Fralon noted some "English go home" graffiti on dustbins in the Périgord, and how the depth of resentment increased in 2006 when the French press uncovered that sixty of the 7,000 fraudulent benefit claimants in the entire département were British. As anyone familiar with our tabloids will know, the idea of scrounging migrants, even in relatively tiny numbers, is one of the most provocative topics there is.

From my own observations, any discontent from the French was largely overshadowed by the infighting of the Brits themselves. Those who'd already made the move appeared to feel threatened by a mass invasion of armchair Francophiles knowing nothing about the country apart from the price of the property. Some writers made snide references to our rich depository of regional stereotypes to drive home the point, relying on the reader to nod and grimace at Lichfield's metaphor of *a slice of the home counties parachuted into the Périgord*, for example. On the other hand, being a Midlander, I felt an obligation to be affronted by Mail on Sunday journalist Lauren Booth[6], when she raised her eyebrows at the possibility – *Gosh* – of *Brummie mummies in the local supermarché, buying ketchup to put on their magret*.

All of this helps to reinforce the caricature of the dependent Brit clinging to their British ways, and it's easy to join in with mocking our embarrassing compatriots. They are not like us! Yet stereotyping is all about over-generalising. I already had an idea of this supposedly typical British incomer in France, but as I moved around the Ariège talking to the incomers, the caricature became more defined as the incomers ranted against it. I could understand how this kind of thinking is a way to

---

6   *Mind your hubcaps, monsieur … the English class war is here.* Mail on Sunday, March 7 2004.

make sense of one's own situation as an English incomer in France, particularly when one moves to the notorious hotspots such as Brittany and Dordogne. It's a way to build imaginary boundaries between who we think we are, and those we want to stand distinct from. But what happens where the British incomers are thin on the ground, as in the Ariège Pyrenees? Do people still complain that the Brits dotted around this under populated region *don't integrate properly*? Surely the Ariège would be a million miles away from what the columnists termed *English suburbia gone badly wrong*?

The Ariège département is about as far south as you can go before hitting Spain or Andorra. Formerly within the Midi-Pyrénées, the département now lies within the recently-formed *Occitanie région* of south-west France. Unlike the honey pots of Dordogne, where the existing incomers seem afraid that newcomers will dilute the French culture they've come to enjoy, the rural and depopulated Ariège is, both physically and metaphorically, miles away from the property magnet of *Dordogneshire*. So I'd been surprised to find the same bickering expressed online among English incomers in this little-known and remote corner of France. According to Tina, one of the incomers I spoke with, Ariège is 'the last place to go in France really, there's not a lot left, is there?' And there was the same sense of being a territorial pioneer. 'I'm not sure where I'll go when they all get here.'

Of course the attraction of France for a new life is nothing new to the British. Peter Thorold's book *The British in France* sets the current phenomenon into its historical context, going into exhaustive detail about who, when and where. Around the time of the Napoleonic wars, for example, many British artisans moved to France as it was easier to earn a living there. When the peace of Amiens failed, many of them were sent to detention centres. The centre at Verdun developed into a facsimile of an English town, where the 1100 detainees were free to open shops, join the Jockey Club and patronise the English church, as well as marry French spouses. After the battle of Waterloo, a developing *entente* brought English artisans and professionals to Paris, and English industrialists were sought elsewhere to set up cotton mills. Many of these earlier settlers lived in small towns for commercial reasons, while others came to buy the kind of extensive property that they could no longer afford in Britain, since estates in France might cost around a third to a quarter of their equivalent back home.

The Pyrenees in particular became a magnet for the English during the 19th century. Travel accounts portrayed it as a mysterious and undiscovered landscape, drawing plant collectors, geologists, hunters and climbers as well as general travellers. In fact, the man regarded as the greatest Pyrenean mountaineer, Charles Packe, was an Englishman, whose 1862 *A Guide to the Pyrenees* is still in print today. Pau in particular became known as an English colony, with its spa drawing those who were convalescing as well as the seekers of exotic flora, fauna and landscape. Traces of the "colony" are still visible in the names of the *rue des Anglais* and a *quartier des Anglais*. Even then it was criticised for what some saw as a transplanting of English customs and social habits, including fox hunting in the surrounding area. There were also substantial English communities building up along the cosmopolitan Riviera, with Nice, for instance, having a range of English churches, doctors, banks, libraries and shops at the end of the 19th century. And just as we have nicknames and clichés of the French, so they developed the same for the English. One occasionally comes across the term *Rosbifs*, from our apparent obsession with a meat that we found annoyingly expensive in France, and Thorold brings in the delightful military term of *hermit crabs*, reflecting the French perspective of an English soldier's tendency to move in and take over other people's property. It was a metaphor that some might feel is just as relevant today in certain areas.

In some respects, today's influxes are seen as a continuation, as a more modern kind of exploitation of France by the "Ryanair crowd" flooding in to snap up French property bargains and sit around drinking like neo-colonials. Yet the idea that the incomers are mostly wealthy or in retirement is a myth. As in the past, there are Britons whose professional expertise invites them to live and work in France, such as the Airbus workers in Toulouse, for instance. What's more, only around half of the British citizens living in France are aged fifty and over, and this percentage is actually lower than that in Spain, Portugal and Bulgaria, according to a report compiled by the Office for National Statistics from Eurostat data.[7] The number of British children living in France is correspondingly higher too. Incomers aged 65+ make up just 19% of the total of around 157,000 Britons living in France. All of this suggests that a significant number of the estimated total will be earning a living, or at least attempting to.

In his survey of British migration to France, Thorold saw two fundamental differences between the older influxes and the 'new breed' of those coming to France over the last thirty or so years. One is that the newer arrivals show a distinct longing to be accepted by the French, compared with their historical counterparts. Of everything that I came away with after my time spent among the Ariège incomers, it was an impression of an overwhelming obsession with being seen to be integrated, and that this was responsible for the infighting between the old-timers and the newcomers. The second difference is the draw of the exotic versus that of the familiar. The 19th-century incomers

---

7   *What information is there on British migrants living in Europe?* January 2017.

to the Pyrenees came seeking the unfamiliar, yet many of today's incomers claim that they are attracted by a France that they think is "like England in the 1950s". That England of the past is now out of their reach, since the few remaining pockets of English rural idyll are largely unaffordable for many. Similarly, the French journalist Fralon concluded that many moves to the Dordogne had been driven by nostalgia; the English might talk about their "love of France", but it is really a longing to return to a more spacious and peaceful England of the past. 'If the English want to breathe,' he claimed, 'they need to emigrate.'

Fralon identifies three distinct "waves" of more recent English incomers to the Périgord that can more or less be applied to other regions of France. The first influx took place during the late 60s, and certainly in the Ariège this has been linked to the arrival of "hippy" or alternative incomers, many of whom have not moved on. This was followed by another wave during the late 1970s, one that was marked more by arrivals who needed to find some kind of paid employment in France. The third wave from the late 1980s was boosted by what Fralon, with his fondness for invasion metaphor, calls the "Blitzkrieg" of the low-cost airlines flying into previously tiny airports. But the bargain seekers were not simply taking advantage of low-cost flights for their summer holidays. Fralon notes that the number of signed property purchases – *actes de vente* – by Britons in 2000 had doubled by 2004 to over 30,000. The Brits were now accounting for 41% of foreign property purchases in France.

Moving to France (or Spain, or the Algarve) for a better life is clearly a different kind of migration compared with those who relocate for better work opportunities or to escape political turmoil. Yet academics, with their fixation on conceptualising everything, have struggled to define it, since surely all migrants are seeking a better life in some way. It's

9

certainly a relatively privileged kind of shift. What else might distinguish this particular movement is that the incomers have a greater flexibility to choose where to live, without being constrained by looking for the best work opportunities. Some academics have characterised it as a peculiarly middle-class phenomenon, whether it's the Brits in France or North Americans in Panama.

I don't wholly agree with this. The endless re-runs of *A Place in the Sun* have brought the idea of going abroad into many homes, and it's not just the middle classes who can act on the dream to sell up and go. The people I met in the Ariège represented a cross-section of British society that could not be lumped en masse into the idea of a financially comfortable, professional, educated middle class. Some *were* comfortable financially, living off income from rental properties, but others were finding it difficult to manage, complaining to me about having to save up to buy petrol for a day trip to the coast. Some reminisced about former high-flying careers in the UK, while others were glad to no longer be on the till in Tesco. One retired couple complained about the lack of decent Ariège restaurants, yet another couple eked out their inadequate pension by growing vegetables and looking around for cleaning jobs, saving up to eat out occasionally.

What was common across the different levels was a keenness to show that they were different from the other Brits. Some looked down upon the "sad" Brits who had to have their English biscuits and bread pudding. Others described themselves as down-to-earth people who admitted to missing the fish and chip shops and went on to sneer at the more pretentious Brits with their poolside aperitifs. It worked both ways, giving everyone an opportunity to show that they were different from the rest, whether they were looking up or down the social scale.

It was the same on the online forum. One of the troublemakers made a derisory comment about hordes of Liverpudlians flying into Carcassonne with Ryanair. Yet at the other end, an angry forum member reminded everyone else that he and his wife, a former cleaner, had worked *f***ing hard* in France, unlike the other *drop-out* English who contributed nothing and were just there for the cheaper property. Whether the sneers were directed upwards at the wealthier classes or downwards at the lower-class bargain seekers, the rants brought in the same old stereotypes. Those fixed caricatures of the British abroad were always there in the background, buzzing around our conversations like a possessed fly. They were an irritating and sometimes uncomfortably close reminder of where people had come from, something that had to be swatted away into that vague mass of other Brits elsewhere.

These caricatures, clichés and stereotypes really are nothing new, harking back to colonial days when the English were renowned for bringing their own customs and clubs into their self-sufficient communities wherever they went. The English were ridiculed by the French for their unintelligible French and their class-based pretentiousness. Referring to the caricatures in today's contexts simply keeps them alive, to be used when your own position as a Brit in France feels a bit shaky. Fralon gives a variation of the same complaint from most of the English incomers he met in Périgord; that it's just not the same anymore now the newer arrivals are here. Fralon's book acknowledges the hypocrisy of the "purist" incomers who want to be "more French than the French", yet he appears to ignore the irony of a couple who themselves had spoken only English on arrival now complaining about how few of the newcomers speak French.

PUSH AND PULL

Ryanair's fondness for opening up routes to obscure French airports has certainly played a role in encouraging Britons to sell up and move to France, but the endless re-runs of overseas property programmes also promote this idea of an escape from the unaffordable and crowded UK. A friend of mine was chatting to a colleague who admitted that he and his wife had a plan to buy a property in France because they "love France". 'Which part of France?' asked the friend. 'Oh I've no idea, we haven't ever been there,' he replied. 'But we love watching the property programmes.'

Reasons for coming to live in France are often divided into two camps: the push and pull factors. In reality they are intertwined. Money is one such factor: I met people who had gained enough capital in their UK property to want to do something with it, pushing them to find something else, but the cheaper prices in France were also a pull factor, enabling them to buy what they'd never be able to afford back in the UK. For some people it was an escape from a boring retirement, or they were looking for a fresh start after a divorce, or something to do once the children had left home. I'd heard people say that Britain was now depressing, or they wanted to escape certain aspects of modern life – the 24/7 existence, as one forum member called it. But all of these push factors went hand in hand with an awareness of what was available: the pull factors described within the books they'd read, the television programmes they'd been wowed by and the property adverts. In spite of the Ariège being seen as somewhere to live a simpler, less consumerist life, where the weather was (sometimes) better and life felt safer, in some ways it was just another commodity. Although the people I spoke to had very different reasons for the move, they'd all been swayed by knowing what was available to them out here in France. Just pick up any copy of a publication such as *French Property News* and the purchase of property is presented as a fantasy, but one that's nevertheless achievable: *Make your dream of buying in France a reality.* Beyond the property, the lifestyle itself is presented as a consumer product. The food commodities associated with rural France are shown in glorious colour: a bounty of fresh fruits and vegetables on the markets, rack after rack of wine, all glamorous and plentiful but not too exotic. And there's the smiling couple raising a glass at the shaded dining table laid with places for visiting family or their new friends. The lifestyle is as tangible a commodity as the properties for sale.

THEN COMES THE BOOK...

While the popular accounts written by incomers provide fodder for armchair dreamers, there's no doubt that this relocation genre has also triggered a domino effect among readers who've dared to follow suit. Peter Mayle's *A Year in Provence* is perhaps the most famous of them all, and this book has certainly been responsible for triggering some of the relocations to the Ariège. This is despite the area's attractions being very different from those of Provence. One woman I spoke to put the entire move down to her husband's dream 'to be that man with the millstone'. Another confessed that buying bikes to fetch the daily baguette was the first thing that they did, although they ended up being too busy working to take the time out to cycle to the *boulangerie*.

Mayle himself continued to produce a string of follow-ups about life in Provence, shrugging off the accusations of never-ending repetition. As he claimed, the topic is such a rich vein, why stop mining it? And so on it goes. Committing your story to print seems to have become firmly entrenched as the next step after the move itself. Incomers continue to publish their accounts, describing the pleasures, the contrast with the former corporate life, and, just as importantly, the crises suffered along the way. As with more conventional travel books, the *Moving to France* narrative is often an account of endurance, but rather than focusing on the process of getting there, the relocation genre dramatises the everyday struggles of a whole new life among unfamiliar language and customs.

Many of these books have a structure that follows broadly similar lines: first the house is found, and then the reader is led through the agonisingly complex bureaucracy of the French purchasing process. This is followed by the renovation of a wreck into a glorious home, and perhaps the stress of running a business such as a vineyard. All of this is moulded into a rollercoaster by adding various debacles, near-catastrophes and the ubiquitous tradesmen who are either too laid-back or incompetent. By including these mishaps, the writer shows how hard they've had to work at overcoming the struggles of a new life in a foreign country. The reader can imagine themselves in such a scenario and share the relief when it all works out in the end.

Some have criticised the genre for a tendency to patronise the French. Mayle himself has been accused of caricaturing them, and it's true that the French locals are often presented as a kind of alien "other", to be gently mocked and satirised. Yet the desire to be accepted by them is paramount, so there's usually an event of some kind that symbolises the eventual embracing of the incomers by the French community.

These narratives are written from a very individual perspective – the "look at what I did" recount – through which their experiences are filtered and embellished for the reader's entertainment. They are clearly popular for readers who enjoy living the fantasy in a kind of virtual way, squirming as they read yet again about the roof collapsing or another embarrassing miscommunication.

Clichés aside, there are some worthy and enjoyable books out there but they nevertheless cast this dream of France in a particular, often predictable, way. Ignoring any references to baguettes, berets or wine, I set out to violate the dream and discover how the English really do manage their new lives in France.

English or British? These aren't interchangeable terms, of course, and there are incomers from all over the UK living in France, not just those who came from England. I've used the term *English* when referring specifically to the Ariège dwellers whom I interviewed, because they were all English. No Scottish, Welsh or Northern Irish, nor ethnic minorities, happened to present themselves for interview, and I didn't come across any during the years of my research. This means that the book focuses on a more defined national group – the English – rather than the broader classification of the British. At other times I refer to the *British* or the *Brits*, and this is because the book takes account of the Brits in France as a wider phenomenon than just the people I came across in the Ariège. The media articles, the forum posts and the interviewees themselves use these terms, and I quote them as used.

ARIÈGE, MORE HOUSES THAN PEOPLE

'*Ariège, une terre sauvage, hein?*' I agreed with the taxi driver that the Ariège is, indeed, a wild place. There had been a slogan used in the past, '*Ariège, terre courage*', which to me reflected the degree of fortitude needed to live here, as well as the bravery of the Ariégeois in sheltering and leading so many to safety over the Pyrenees in the Second World War. According to the Holocaust Museum in Paris, 446 locals had been deported from the département, which was a significant number when you consider that the pre-war population in 1936 stood at 155,134. It was a ratio of approximately one deportee to every 350 inhabitants.

That's not to say that the entire département has yet to be tamed by progress. Driving past the faceless business parks that frame the autoroutes of the northern, flatter Ariège, you could be anywhere at all in France. Over to the east, the towns of Foix, Tarascon and Mirepoix are managing to maintain their individual character, although they remain charmingly small; the population of Foix, the administrative town of the Ariège, has not quite reached the 10,000 mark.

It's at the western end of the Ariège where the wildness has stubbornly taken root, in an area still known by its former designation as the Couserans. Although the name no longer has any official or administrative status, it maintains a lingering cultural significance and romantic association with the wilder and depopulated western Ariège. No less than eighteen rivers radiate from the Couserans Pyrenees, their twisting valleys sheltered by thickly forested hills that rise steeply up to the higher mountain areas. Venturing above the tree line brings you to rolling green pastures where, in summer, you step in time to the chime of the bells around the necks of the cattle. These bucolic landscapes eventually give way to vast grey expanses of boulder rubble, where clear water barely ripples as it lies in the hollows gouged by long-ago glaciers, and hundreds of other tiny lakes break up the greyness as they reflect the sky.

A Couserans builder explained to me why he was so busy by summing it up as a place with more houses than people. Around a quarter of the houses in the Ariège are second homes, although the percentage is much higher in some of the Couserans villages. More than 50% of the houses in communes such as Massat and Seix are holiday residences, but it is more like 80% in Ustou and Couflens. Many of these are occupied during the short summer season by families who have long since moved away but return for weekends and holidays, while others are rented out. Even with relatively low numbers, the summer and winter faces of the villages could differ immensely. I met a number of English incomers who'd settled in and around the small town of Seix, for example, which has a population of just 842, although in summer its narrow lanes are swelled by a further 1200 or so holidaymakers. When the season was over, some of the restaurants stayed closed for more than half of the year.

These old houses of the Couserans had usually been built at the time of a rapid population increase in the mid 18th century, although it was an expansion that was short-lived, since the area's resources could not sustain the growing number of inhabitants. There followed a steady population decline, most keenly seen in the mountain areas with their chronic unemployment and associated poverty. There was also loss due to epidemics and the First World War; the latter alone accounted for a decline by 13% of the Ariège population.

Nevertheless there *are* people living there today, and they are slowly offsetting the population decline. Despite the continuing haemorrhage of young people to find work, a gentle increase in incomers is cancelling the loss so that, paradoxically, Ariège is now one of the fastest growing départements in France. Much of this demographic recovery is concentrated in the northern, more urbanised areas, although it's also taking place in some smaller, isolated mountain communities. The effects, however, are very different between the two. The "golden triangle" of the towns of Pamiers, Saverdun and Mazerès is reportedly thriving from the influx of working people, while the arrival of many retirees to the rural south-west seems less sustainable, as it does little to stem the ageing of the population in *communes* where a third, on average, are past working age.

Yet not all arrivals are retirees. The Couserans in particular has seen an influx of what the French call the *neo-ruraux*, or even *marginaux*; what some still refer to as "hippies". This incursion began in the late 1960s, with an international mix of incomers who came seeking an alternative way to live. This reputation never really went away, which means that incomers are still arriving in search of a life that's partly or wholly off-grid. It's a return to the land, although it results in little outward change on the landscape, since any "farming" remains firmly at subsistence level. At the same time it's helping to stem the depopulation trend. As the mayor of Massat put it, the original long-haired *neo-ruraux* may now have succumbed to baldness, but their children continue to enliven the schools.[8]

Ariège still lags well behind the more popular areas of Dordogne and Brittany for British incomers, although the arrival *d'un grand nombre de Britanniques* in the former Midi-Pyrénées region has been noted by French statisticians.[9] Thousands arrived in the former Midi-Pyrénées region between 2001 and 2006, but in the Ariège itself they made up less than 30% of the foreign incomers. This is much lower than the Lot and the Gers départements, for example, where the Brits make up over 45% of foreign incomers.[10] It's a growing number of Dutch, Belgian and German incomers who've augmented the dwindling Ariège population, yet it's the British *vague,* or "wave", that's been singled out by the statisticians, particularly around Mirepoix.

8   http://www.paysdelours.com/fr/communes-adet/massat/histoire.html
9   Simonnet et al. (2008). Ariège.
10 Touret, L., Bourniquel, C., & Poisson, C. (2010). *L'espace rural en Mi-di-Pyrénées: dynamique démographique et accès aux équipements.*

One of the motivations for this book was to question why the English incomers had chosen to settle here. Sometimes the reasons were startling as they reflected a total lack of knowledge of the place. It became common to hear an incomer say that they had never even heard of the Ariège before they were persuaded by an estate agent to visit the département and view a house that "ticks all of your boxes". I got the impression that for many people it really was about finding the right house. The specific town, village or region, and sometimes even the actual *country*, seemed to be low on the list of priorities. Almost everyone I spoke to mentioned property prices, suggesting that the aim of getting the most for your money had led some people to end up in this lesser-known corner of France, rather than the Aude next door that had more sun and less rain. *It's good value for money... our property in the UK bought us a lot more here.* But was it a blinkered perspective, fuelled by television programmes that encourage buyers to think only of getting more for their money? These programmes skim over the day-to-day aspects of a new life in a totally unfamiliar area. A detached house that ticks all the boxes, and for less than a pokey terrace in Bolton!

This isn't to suggest that finding "the right house" is only based on getting value for money. A French researcher, Aude Etrillard, who was similarly fascinated by the incoming Britons around north-west France, has analysed six books written in this very English *relocation to France* genre. Etrillard concluded that in all cases, the central character was the house itself, symbolising a strong emotional connection between house and writer. Of course these are books written to entertain, and it's fun to describe falling in love with a house and the subsequent ups and downs of the relationship. For those who bought the first and only house they viewed, it really was love at first sight, rather than a hard-headed ticking of boxes. Even Peter Mayle described seeing his house in Provence one afternoon and mentally moving in by dinner, with one of its main attractions being its location within a national park that protected it from "the creeping horrors of property development".

Whether practical or emotional, it's all propped up by the marketing forces. Digital technology in particular has made it much easier to find out about available property in a place you haven't yet visited. Online forums for "expats" make it easy to ask other incomers about life when you have little idea of what you are coming to. Some of the questions asked by newcomers on the Ariège forum indicated they had only a basic familiarity with the Ariège region, perhaps gained from a holiday or two, or even just from surfing the internet. New members referred to themselves as *newbies* and talked about how they were looking forward to becoming fluent in French, as if it was that simple. English isn't widely spoken in the Ariège and I wondered how they'd manage in the early years.

I guessed that the existence of an online forum for English speakers went some way towards giving people confidence that they'd get the help they needed when they arrived. It was clear from the posts that some members viewed the forum as a kind of crutch to support them as they made the big move, asking about where their children could go to school and hoping that an English-speaking doctor would exist somewhere. Some of the newcomers were like sponges, passively absorbing whatever information was thrown at them as they requested members to *please keep any advice coming*. I detected an air of desperation when one newcomer implored that *all advice [is] appreciated, good or bad*. Was that just a careless, throwaway comment, or was their lack of knowledge so profound that even bad advice would be welcome, just as long as someone was prepared to tell them *something*?

All of this drove me to find some of the people behind these voices and to hear their stories for myself. A starting point was to find out if the English really knew what they were coming to when they uprooted themselves to this depopulated corner of France. The rural Ariège is a long, long way from the vineyards and gastronomy of Mayle's Provence and what Etrillard described as an English fetishisation of French lifestyle. Restaurants closed on a summer Saturday? Bars closing at 8pm in summer? To some people, Ariège is 'the back of beyond'. Surely it would be easier to settle in the popular plains of the neighbouring Aude, perhaps around Carcassonne or towards Perpignan, or even a little further north to the Lot and its *canard*-with-everything menus?

The Ariège landscape is wonderful for walking but those drawn to the idea of old-fashioned community might be spooked to see so many abandoned and decaying houses littering the wooded foothills. I've met drivers, both English and French, who are unnerved by the twisting narrow roads that chase the rivers and then rise precipitously along high ground. The English often cite our weather as a reason to move to France, but Ariège dwellers will need to find something positive in a month when it rains every day, especially when it's August. And anyone who feels uneasy with the mix of people, including the pierced and dreadlocked *neo-ruraux* with their battered vans, might feel a bit out of place.

So the Ariège could be an odd choice for a Francophile, as at times it can feel very much apart from the rest of France. Events of history, plus the landscape and the geographical proximity to the Spanish frontier, have left the département with an enduring association with sanctuary and resistance – what Edward Stourton refers to as an unmistakeable *genus loci*, or spirit of the place, in a most secretive region.[11] It had

11   Cruel crossing: Escaping Hitler across the Pyrenees (2013).

been a place of sanctuary for the Cathars in the 13th century, and many thousands of Spanish republicans fled Franco to take refuge in France, making their way over the Ariège Pyrenees. Shortly after this was the flow in the opposite direction of those evading the Nazis and the Vichy government, with many escape lines once again passing through the Ariège over the Pyrenees into Spain. The decades of depopulation and the influx of retirees and *neo-ruraux* have done little to change the landscape, and even now there are dark valleys and secluded villages that seem utterly detached from the 21st century.

The area's aptitude for concealing fugitives wasn't just confined to wartime. One particular house perched above Massat had been the final hiding place of Xavier Fortin and his two sons, a fugitive trio who fled from the boys' mother in 1998 when the children were aged six and seven. Evading the mother's attempts to track them down, they criss-crossed the country, living a nomadic existence among communes, tipis and borrowed apartments until they finally arrived in Massat in 2007 and lived in a secluded spot until their discovery in February 2009. It was a sensational story for the media, who descended on Massat so they could tell the world about this wild valley where a man and his children could hide from the law, undisturbed. I expect journalists were delighted when they tracked down the ramshackle barn that had been home to the fugitives, seeing visual evidence that would add to the implication of child deprivation and illiteracy. Images showing the barn from the most unflattering angle – above – looked down on the misshapen tin sheets that formed a roof, and the only colour to liven the dreariness of winter was the white of a few chickens and the melting snow. Bearded locals who'd been happy to assist the family suddenly became unhelpful when faced with the reporters, smiling as their city cars skidded around in the snow. The *maire* of Massat, perhaps mindful that his commune was getting a reputation for sheltering criminal savages, went on record to insist that the family was friendly and open, as well as educated. The boys and their father subsequently wrote a book about their experience, which has been made into a film: *Vie Sauvage*.

An empty landscape is not just useful for evading the law, as it can also bring a sense of liberation to anyone who takes the trouble to walk it. That emptiness can also be hugely inconvenient, as public transport is non-existent in some areas and at times the lack of people can feel creepy. One August Saturday lunchtime we strolled around the town of St Lizier, one of the most historical towns of the region and on the UNESCO World Heritage list, looking for somewhere – anywhere – to eat. We eventually gave up, marvelling that the only person we'd seen was a woman lying asleep on a bench.

The famous GR10 long-distance path across the length of the Pyrenees crosses through the Ariège with a number of extensions and diversions, all spectacular, but the emptiness of the landscape has often caused problems for hikers; some GR10-ers have been known to buy a tent on entering the Ariège, or miss it out altogether. Even Nicholas Crane missed the opportunity to describe the Ariège section on his epic walk across the mountains of Europe; one chapter ends with walking down into the green Ariège, and the next chapter takes up the walk over the border in Pyrenees-Orientales.[12] The lack of tourist accommodation in the Couserans might encourage incomers to plan a business from renting out gîtes, but the reality is a very short season of perhaps 4–5 months per year.

Yet incomers who deliberately seek isolation will find no end of options in terms of hard-to-reach villages, hidden hamlets or even one of the houses that the estate agents advise can only be reached on foot. The higher up you go, the

---

12   Clear Waters Rising (1996).

narrower and more decrepit the road or track, but the longer the sun shines on your house. And in the lowlands there are many attractions for a certain kind of person. Members of the online forum made it sound like a wise choice. One woman who'd lived there for five years encouraged another who was thinking about it by saying: *It is a great place to live, the locals are friendly and the air non-polluted and just a wonderful area to live all year round. Your children will benefit from one of the most beautiful areas of France.* People talked about the slower way of life in an area that was a little behind the times, summarising it as a *low-population area of France with marvellous natural history and a laid-back attitude.* The forum gave barely any indication that it wasn't always ideal for a new life, but there was enough evidence of people leaving to show that the Ariège didn't suit everyone. I suspected that for people who'd invested financially and emotionally in the big move, it would be an embarrassing loss of face to admit that they'd made the wrong decision.

A HOUSE AT THE END OF A TRACK

The first time I drove into the Ariège I crossed the baking plains of the Aude into what gradually became a humid jungle; the steep wooded hillsides steamed as the morning rains evaporated in the heat of the August afternoon, the air lying trapped and oppressive within the valley. My eyes scanned the green for signs of habitation, marvelling at the huddles of old houses in shades of brown that were livened by the occasional rebel in dull pink. How different it felt in November, when the foothills had taken on their brown winter coat to accept the coming snows. The car swung around the tight bends of the Col de Port, past what I'd always assumed were abandoned houses – yet at dusk they awoke, their dull lights hinting of life behind the windows as the tang of wood smoke wafted into the car.

That November I'd just signed away a moderate inheritance in return for a set of keys to an old stone house in the Couserans that had the date of 1876 carved roughly into the lintel above the door. The house maintained a refrigerator-like temperature indoors throughout the year, which made a useful saving on anything as fancy as air conditioning during the high summer heat. The exterior walls, built of stone, appeared to be counting down a half-life, as on exceptionally hot days I watched uneasily as clumps of baked mud mortar pinged off into the grass. The roof was covered with roughly hewn slates and heavy stones known as *lauzes*. It was a house with no right angles, a skewed parallelogram positioned to catch the most of the sun before it disappeared behind the hill opposite. This was another bonus, as its height meant that the sun warmed the stone a good hour or so longer than those sitting in the valley. Walking back from a long walk on a still-warm evening, I would catch the scent of dry heat radiating from the old stones, and I would spend a few moments sitting there, with my back to the wall, letting the warmth massage my aching shoulders.

The house had been wedged into the hillside at the end of a brittle track that was little wider than a car. It sat above an ambitiously named "parking" area, where a slip of the foot during the seven-point turn might easily nudge a car over into the steep wooded ravine. Some years after moving in I was told that this had already happened twice – to the postman and to a previous occupant of my house. The postman had survived. I was told not to worry; the other driver had been under the influence, but I began to experiment with parking the car down in the valley. It meant a walk of 21 minutes up and 19 minutes down a sodden path along the river, but I grew fond of the walk, stepping carefully to avoid the colourful fire salamanders that had made their home in the damp foliage.

The hamlet had just three houses. The adjacent house was an almost derelict and little visited holiday home, although the third house was occupied all year round by Vincent and Juliette. Their house lay just down the slope so that my windows were level with its chimneys, and my house often filled with the tang of their wood fires. Unlike most of the houses where I visited the English incomers, mine lacked the two things that the English seemed fixated on: privacy and a proper garden. Although the house was perched above a dead-end track, a few people regularly toiled past on their way up to a barn higher up the hillside, glancing in and waving as they passed my window. They always carried huge rucksacks. I never found out what they were carrying or why the packs were always stuffed full on the way up as well as down. It felt impolite to ask.

Most of the time the window was filled with a close-up view of the other side of the narrow valley. A forested spur lay directly opposite, a huge pyramid that blocked out much of the sky, although it was a useful indicator of the seasons. After the trees opposite became thickened by spring, the dense green of summer would shift to a faded brown, when leaves carpeted the ground, and previously hidden buildings and pathways became visible again through the skeletal branches. At any time of the year there could be days when curtains of mist slunk up the valley to block the view, making it easy to imagine a horizon that was endless, not just a mere stone's throw.

On an indoors day I would be drawn to the window, sitting in front of it to paint the view or write, my eyes moving from the forest outside to the wooden panelling that surrounded the interior walls. People frowned when they came into the house and gazed around at the extent of the chestnut panelling that the previous owners – a visiting family of hunters – had used to disguise the jagged edges and disintegrating mud mortar of the old stone walls. I just shrugged when they asked me if I liked it. In truth I'd never really given much thought to the inner decor, but I grew accustomed to it. If anything, the panelling was a natural domestication of what was visible out of my window.

Looking diagonally from one edge of the window to the other, I could see a minor summit rearing its head beyond the forested pyramid. This peak of Tuc de la Coume was the first thing I looked for each morning; if it was clear, the first light of sunrise would illuminate the upper section with gold. In late September it became a rusty orange, followed by the bare rock of autumn before the snows. One August I awoke to see the peak dusted with a thin layer of icing sugar snow that was gone by nightfall. When the true snows came, they remained stubbornly on its pinnacle, drawing attention to the peak against the winter-coated forest.

Although the house had nothing recognisable as a "garden", it came with some fairly useless bits of land scattered around, a common consequence of French inheritance laws that split a property between surviving children. I did have a steep section of slope at the rear, although most of it lay directly behind the house next door. I was baffled to find that I also owned half of a ruin in front of their house, a shell so overgrown with ivy that I hadn't even realised that there were stone walls beneath it. There was a ruined barn adjoining my house but it belonged to Vincent, whilst outside his house was a tract that I owned, a square of weeds where I'd sometimes spotted visitors taking a pee. Eventually the three houses did an exchange, allowing me to swap my distant half-a-ruin for the closer one, which I flattened into a wonky terrace.

Vincent and Juliette seemed typical of the French incomers in this laid-back part of the Pyrenees; people drawn by the lack of rules, who were largely self-sufficient in their old stone houses that seemed to stand without anything resembling mortar. They grew their own food and firewood, and generally helped one another out. Anything resembling a newish car stood out among the dented and daubed Citroen 2CVs, the Renault vans and the odd Citroen DS. I was not surprised that the no-frills Fiat Panda was popular there, but the number of first-generation Pandas was only slowly being outnumbered by the newer models.

Wandering or driving around the Couserans, one is taken by what an English woman described as *a strange mix of people*. One comes across a few remaining Ariégeois, often elderly and always polite, as well as the more alternative incomers. It wasn't uncommon to see a battered van, with cracked windscreen and tattered curtains, parked far from visible signs of habitation, a clue that people were living somewhere in the woods, perhaps a mile or two away.

The area around the town of Massat, known as the Massatois, is perhaps the place most strongly associated with the alternative incomers. Reactions to these *marginaux* seemed mixed; some bemoaned the reputation of the Ariège as an "anything goes" area, as one local confided to me when we stood watching people gyrating and snogging among the more sedate locals on the dance floor at Massat festival. On the whole, however, I felt that attitudes were largely accepting. I'd been told that people had sometimes been allowed to live in empty houses and barns in exchange for basic upkeep; a kind of official squatting that was useful to owners who didn't want the hassle of formal letting and associated maintenance. The *maire* of the commune promotes its motto – *libris et fieris* – free and proud – as genuinely reflecting the spirit of Massat, one that welcomes the incomers for their contribution to rural regeneration where around 40% of the population is aged 60 years and over. No doubt mindful that the alternatives are regarded less positively in some quarters, the *maire* speaks positively of them and encourages others to be more accepting and supportive of those who have chosen a different way of life, rather than try to exclude them. I liked his use of irony to challenge people to cast off their pre-conceptions and *dare to meet the Massatois; do not be afraid: even "hippy-communists" aren't savages!*[13]

Hand in hand with these associations comes another, that of marijuana. A few years back I'd been proudly shown around a tiny vegetable plot that had the tell-tale plants interspersed among the tomatoes, all part of subsistence. I'd once overheard a visitor asking where they could buy some, and the reply, in shocked tones, that it wasn't grown to *sell*. An envelope was duly passed to them without any money exchanging hands. Undoubtedly some growers did sell it, and the occasional news item about raids on marijuana crops never failed to exploit the town's association with the "hippy" incomers of 1968.

The daughter of one such couple has been busy writing up her memories of being brought up as one of eight 'wild children' near Massat. Djalla-Marie Longa was born to a German mother who arrived in the 60s with a dog and a guitar, and then settled down in determined non-conformity with a French partner. The family lived in Figuets, "a hamlet like no other", with candlelight, no running water and no plastic toys; the children weren't schooled but instead worked on the subsistence farm, and transport was a horse-drawn cart. Clothing was whatever they managed to make, although the mother herself, sporting a curtain of hennaed hair, sometimes rebelled against the social norm of getting dressed. Djalla-Marie became a rebel herself at 16, but it was a resistance against the way of life enforced by her parents, as she became

---

13   http://www.paysdelours.com/fr/communes-adet/massat/massat.html

drawn to what she knew of the other life "down below". Now a business owner in Massat, she balances some of the family's ideological values with a little comfort – using solar panels but driving a car, for example – and aspects of her wild upbringing have been woven into books that combine fact and fiction: *Mon enfance sauvage* (2011) and *Terre Courage* (2013).

Most of the English incomers I met raised their eyebrows when I mentioned that I came from near Massat, probably wondering just to what extent I fit in with the local population. 'Massat... that's another strange place.' 'Apparently there's an awful lot of drugs growing in Massat.' 'I think over at Massat you have smoking parties, don't you?' They visibly relaxed when I positioned myself closer to their social world; this was easily done by referring to the smokers as "them" rather than "we". To be fair I'd never been offered a smoke of anything, perhaps being seen as too square, although I'd come away from social gatherings feeling the effect of hours of passive inhalation. The closest I got was being offered an absinthe-like spirit from a bottle stuffed with marijuana leaves. The pourer reassured me that it wouldn't make me high, just happy.

Although I occasionally catch the tang of marijuana whilst wandering around, there are two other particular aromas that I associate with the Ariège. Catching a whiff of either of them brings me sharply into focus on where I am. The first is the scent from the Himalayan balsam (*impatiens glandulifera*) plant, whose flashes of pink along the verges indicate that water is close by. This invasive plant, native to the Himalayas, has been vigorous in its colonisation of the Couserans verges, often growing to waist height. Walking or cycling around in the summer months, its perfume is almost always there, infusing the air beyond the clusters of trumpet-shaped pink flowers that are distinctively attached by a stem at the top of the "trumpet" rather than the end. The balsam is fond of damp woodland and the banks of watercourses, which is why it has taken root so vigorously along the river valleys. The very fact that it grows close to water facilitates its multiplication, as its explosive pods can shoot seeds up to 7 metres away, meaning that they easily get carried away by the water as well as on the tyres of vehicles. Before I knew what it was I liked its colour and perfume, and I was right to assume that people had deliberately planted it for aesthetic reasons. But it had turned out to be a pest, not only because of its vigorous seed dispersal, but there is also a worry that it leads to erosion of the riverbanks, due to its flimsy root system that leaves the edges vulnerable over the winter die-back. In ecologically sensitive areas such as riverbanks, its dense growth could easily overwhelm native species, and there is an added danger that the density of growth might impede water flow during high rainfall, leading to increased risk of flooding. I knew that in Devon and other areas they organised "Balsam bashing" days to stem the reproduction. Recommendations and work were taking place in the Ariège to try and eradicate *la balsamine de l'Himalaya,* but it needed to be carried out extensively and methodically if it was going to work.

The other odour is harder to define, and it's characterised by the smell of smoke and of things smoked – the tang of the wood fires with their silver plumes curling above heavy stone roofs, as well as the rich odour of smoked meats and the scent of clothes dried in front of the fire. I inhaled it when I got close to people, but I also caught it when walking past an open doorway. I know that Juliette's daughter had suffered some teasing at school from other girls who told her she "smelled of the fire". I was pretty certain that I also left a similar trail in my wake. It wasn't unpleasant, and for me it embodied the Ariège way of life.

This book has grown out of an academic study that began to take shape on that hot day standing at the crossroads, trying to make sense of Gerald's directions. Yet I knew that these stories would resonate with a much wider audience than the insular world of academia. Much of the existing writing about the Brits in France refers to stereotypes, but I wanted to listen to individual stories and try to work out *how* these clichés collided with people's own experiences. Readers will recognise some of the characteristics that are said to typify the Brits in France: the difficulties in speaking French, the hankering after English foods and the reliance on each other. The Brits have been dismissed as a cliquey and dependent bunch, good for little more than mockery. As one angry forum member ranted, *you are all lost sheep in a huge field.* Yet as time went on I became more and more drawn into the contradiction between their rants against the "other" Brits in France, and the way that they nevertheless relied on each other. The more I listened, the more I understood the conflict between what they said they believed, and what they told me they did. People try to understand their own place here in France, and if their stories sometimes appear hypocritical, then I see that as a symptom of living under the shadow of a stereotype.

The house at the end of the track is both a literal place and a metaphor. The book was written whilst gazing out from a house perched above the end of a dilapidated track with a green stripe of grass running between the potholes. I met others who were also living at the end of a track, enjoying sizeable gardens and privacy that they could never have afforded back in England. But some, like Gerald, deliberately avoided that isolation, choosing to live in a village centre for what it offered in terms of a more active social integration. For them, the end of the track was the metaphorical end of the journey to the Ariège; sometimes planned in detail, more often the result of a whim. And for some it was just one journey before the next one began.

1

HAVE A PHOTOGRAPH
TAKEN WITH THE ENGLISH

AN ENGLISHMAN ABROAD

Having finally located Gerald, standing on the pavement outside his small townhouse, we walked though the garage to a courtyard where a table was laid with tea and biscuits. I was glad for the shade provided by the house and the courtyard walls. September was coming to a close but temperatures were still rising, to reach 27 degrees centigrade later that week, followed by an unbroken run of sunshine well into the middle of October. Driving around, visiting the friendly Brits to chat and drink tea in their gardens, it was the easiest thing to agree with them about what a glorious place they'd moved to. Hardly anyone mentioned that July and August had seen more rainy days than dry ones.

'There's always this thing about an Englishman abroad. You have a kind of freedom, what the Germans call *narrenfreiheit*; it means the jester's freedom to mock the king. I've got this freedom as a foreigner, kind of a liberation thing. If you like, I can dip into French society.' Outwardly, Gerald appeared to have it all. He and his wife Sandra, who was temporarily back in England, were in their sixties and retired. They'd bought a house in the unfamiliar Ariège after visiting a friend in the neighbouring département. He waved his arm around the dappled courtyard of the townhouse, intent on not being seen as a dreamer seeking a Mayle-style rural retreat. 'Look at this house, it's not your French idyll is it, the lovely gîte at the end of the track, in the middle of nowhere. It's not that.' Choosing a townhouse was all part of the kind of incomer they wanted to be, and to be seen as. The fact that it *wasn't* a house at the end of a track was as significant to Gerald as rural idyll was to some of the others. Choosing a townhouse that opened onto the street, in a small town where passers-by would stop and chat, was all part of the story of how he and Sandra found themselves integrated "astonishingly quickly". Both Gerald and his wife spoke French, the kind learned through formal education. 'But I speak it like a book, like a Voltaire, you know.'

After talking about dipping into French society, Gerald became more wary of coming across as superficial. He went into detail about his integration, talking about gaining friends for life among the local French, of holding dinner parties, joining clubs and choirs as well as standing in the local election. And all this took place within six months of moving here. 'Yes, we've been really lucky,' he mused. 'Except, having said that, we did make an effort. If you expect French people to beat a path to your door, well, you must be barmy. Why would they?' Anyone reading their way through the relocation-to-France books could well anticipate friendly overtures from the French; you would only have to read Peter Mayle's account of the ceremonial presentation of an enormous stone-hewn primrose-planted antique jardinière, a Christmas gift from neighbours and acquaintances.

34

Gerald quashed such unrealistic ideas. 'I think they're a little suspicious of the English anyway because, in my experience, most of them don't speak very good French. In fact some of the English don't speak *any* French and it amazes me.'

'You know of such people, then?' I asked.

'Personally, yes,' he nodded. 'Why the hell do they come here?'

It was a good question. I'd had an inkling that the media was putting ideas into the heads of people who weren't that familiar with France, let alone the language, but the finer point about why they ended up in the "back of beyond" Ariège was partly answered with his next comment. 'Ariège isn't for the rich,' he mused, which was another way of saying that it offered value for money for Brits seeking a new life in France but who couldn't afford the formulaic dreamlands of Provence or Dordogne. Gerald didn't strike me as the kind of person who'd act on a whim, so I was surprised when he admitted that they'd bought the house on impulse whilst staying with friends near Carcassonne. 'His wife was an estate agent and so we took the plunge but we didn't know the Ariège. I'd never been to the south of France. We had no idea about the area, no idea about the town, but as it turned out it's been lucky.' After using the house as a holiday home, they'd decided to move permanently a few years ago.

I wondered what else Gerald, with his French dinner parties, his Voltaire-like syntax and his council votes, had to say about the other Brits living around and about. I began by asking if he'd used any of the English speakers who offered services locally, such as building and decorating. He shook his head. 'We usually ask around our French friends, if they know anybody, and normally they do.' He did use a nearby English tradesman whose limited French meant that he relied on business from English speakers, but that was because they'd become friends. As the conversation drew on, Gerald became more and more animated about other English incomers. Like many of the English I spoke to out here, Gerald was careful to distance himself from the Brit stereotype. 'They're a sore point with us.' He railed against what he saw as the superficiality of the Brits who come to consume the French way of life, depending on fellow expats for a social life and not giving anything back to the community. 'It just doesn't agree with me, this business of *I'll take the climate and the baguette and the coffee and the café.*' Even lower down the hierarchy were those who continued to eat English food. 'What madness… it's insane… we saw an advert that said: *Stock up your gîte for your English visitors with English food.* Baked beans, who the hell wants that when you can go and have *cassoulet?*' he said, drawing out the word as if he was about to lift up a spoonful of the thick sauce.

'But is there much of that kind of thing here in the Ariège, do you think?' I wondered.

'I don't think there is. But perhaps we don't see them because of our lifestyle.' He went on to describe how he and Sandra actively participated in local protests against teacher redundancies, sitting on the roundabout to disrupt the traffic on the main road. 'We meet other Brits who are also into protests and stuff.' It sounded as if they rarely came across other English incomers, and mostly when they were involved in local protests. Yet as time went on and I moved around talking to the incomers, I came to realise that Gerald and his wife were known to almost all the others whom I met. 'They're lovely,' said Elaine a few weeks later. 'They speak wonderful French, the two of them.'

Apart from the wonderful French, Gerald was also renowned for his sense of humour. An anecdote was later relayed to me about a type of charades played among an English gathering, where Gerald played a convincingly petulant elderly character. As we chatted he brought up this side of his character as something particularly English. 'I like trying to amuse the French,' he admitted, 'and one of the things about the English is our relative sense of humour. If you can show one, the French like it. I think they expect the English to be eccentric and have a sense of humour.'

Humour and eccentricity as English traits have been singled out by the anthropologist Kate Fox as important aspects of what she calls an English "collective distinctiveness".[14] On reflection it's a useful way of thinking, because it gives the English in France something more positive to identify with, rather than the usual negative stereotypes. Incomers want to be seen as different, not just mindlessly following the flood of expats over the Channel, but they also want to fit in and be seen as integrated. So if their Englishness stands out in France, that's all right so long as it's all down to their funny English traits of being humorous and eccentric. I was also beginning to see how the concept of *narrenfreiheit*, the ability to get away with things because you're foreign, might work for someone like Gerald. 'You're forgiven because you don't know any better, do you,' he said, 'you don't have to obey the conventions.' As an Englishman abroad he couldn't be blamed for his mistakes, and moreover he could make comedy out of them, as it was all part of his peculiarly English brand of foreignness.

I pondered on what I'd imagined was an air of wistfulness around Gerald, despite the appearance of having everything that would symbolise a successful integration to many other incomers. And despite the positioning of himself as doing things the right way, I wasn't picking up any sense of

---

14   Watching the English (2005).

smugness, although it would have been understandable if he'd come across as self-congratulatory in how things had turned out. I wondered if there was a sense of something missing, perhaps linked to his wife being back in England. I reached for another biscuit and asked him if there were times when he felt less positive about being an outsider, which drew out some frustrations.

'I'm English in culture. Things that you grow up with, all that body of culture that we call "English" is accessible to us, but the French one isn't and that's what we miss out on,' he said. Speaking with Voltaire-like syntax was considerably better than a vocabulary limited to a dozen or so French "keywords", like his English tradesman friend, but it still wasn't good enough for Gerald. 'I don't understand everything and sometimes I get the wrong end of the stick. It's still a foreign language to me and the culture's alien, I haven't grown up with it.'

I was beginning to sense a conflict of emotions. This feeling of otherness didn't always sit comfortably with the liberating feeling of being a foreigner, and it seems to account for why some Britons entrench themselves within English-speaking networks or eventually return to the UK. If incomers feel out of place and unable to share much with the French, it's not surprising when they turn towards the more familiar cultural landscape of their compatriots. For Gerald, who seemed settled in many ways, it equated to a feeling of frustration, of something missing. Similar sentiments were expressed when I later met Susan, who was also competent in the language: 'It's not having been brought up in the culture, things that in England I take for granted. You can't take anything for granted anymore and that's where I feel foreign, I think.'

"Home" was still the north of England, and Gerald's wife Sandra was currently there to visit family, having taken their

38

French neighbours with her to show them around the English countryside. I'd been so engaged in absorbing the long list of activities symbolising their social integration that it was a jolt when Gerald added that Sandra really wanted to be back home. 'She said to me the other week, she doesn't want to stay here. There will be a time when she really wants to be back in the UK and live there permanently.' It was mostly down to missing family, especially grandchildren, but there were other factors. 'This feeling of being at ease with the language when you're at home, that's something we haven't got here.' He admitted that he'd like to keep the house for holidays. 'I'm happy when I'm here, I'm really happy apart from this worry of not being able to communicate one hundred percent effectively. And while Sandra's always having fun here, I don't think I'm misquoting her when I say she doesn't feel a hundred percent herself here.'

I was grateful to Gerald for opening up to me and I understood what he meant. I'd come away from social gatherings myself, knowing that I'd only said what I'd been *able* to say in French, which was not at all the same as what I'd have said if I'd had my mother tongue at my disposal. It left a sense that I wouldn't ever fully know people, nor would people really be able to know me, not in that "hundred percent" way. It's true that some of the incomers came with barely any command of French and seemed happy to get by at a basic level, relying on others when things got complicated. But not everybody was comfortable with that.

Our chat in the dappled courtyard was also the start of what began to emerge as a kind of inner conflict among some of the incomers. Gerald, with his French dinner parties and his scorn towards English food in France, deriding the "sore point" Brits, was nevertheless known to so many of the English out here, even those living on the other side of the Ariège. 'He's brilliant, he's one of our friends from the group,' smiled Elaine when I mentioned his name. Yet people were at pains to be seen as doing the right thing: becoming integrated, speaking French and immersing themselves in French social life. And in order to belong to the *right* side, it was necessary to make it clear what being on the *wrong* side entailed. Gerald's version of superficial incomers who couldn't manage without their baked beans and bread pudding was just the start of what turned out to be an exhaustive account of those vague "other Brits" who lived beyond the pale. Few acknowledged how difficult it might be to abandon everything that one had grown up with and enjoyed.

The teapot and plate of biscuits in front of me were part of an English ritual that had been noted in France long before the recent waves of incomers. The American Mary Waddington visited the "anglicised town" of Hazebrouck in 1916 and raised her eyebrows at the way that English customs such as church services and afternoon tea rituals had been imposed – as the English "always do".[15] Unlike *Dordogneshire*, English-style tearooms were not at all a common feature of the Ariège towns, although there was one that I'd come across in the medieval town of Mirepoix. This was perhaps the Ariège town most notorious for its association with the English, and at that time it was undergoing what the Ariège.com tourism website referred to as the "Dordogne phenomenon". What this meant in tangible terms was the appearance of English estate agencies, English-language menus and the availability of English newspapers and magazines in the town. Mirepoix even had an English church service. The previous week I'd spent a Monday morning wandering around Mirepoix's market, eavesdropping on the small groups of Brits who were gathered here and there, inviting each other for "Apero evenings". It did feel that every other voice was English, despite it being at

15   Peter Thorold

the end of the season, and there would have been many more during the peak summer time. In winter the English voices were greatly diminished, although there'd been a comment on the forum that their continuing presence was a welcome and comforting sound to the year-round residents.

I expect that the British-owned tearoom in the main square was also a haven of comfort, so long as one could make sense of the bizarre mix of English and French chalked onto the A-board. A photograph of the menu was at that time featured on the Mirepoix page of the Ariège.com tourism website, where it was used to illustrate the town's popularity with the Brits. The menu advertised such things as:

Jambon – omelette Spanish
Salads: thon (tuna)
Scones with jam and cream
Bread pudding

Like me, the website organisers had found the muddle of French and English too funny to ignore, admitting to me that it had made them snigger. I expect they eventually realised that poking fun at the crown jewel of Mirepoix was not the wisest move for a site whose *raison d'être* was promoting tourism, as the photograph and the references to the "Dordogne phenomenon" have since disappeared from the page. Yet that image of the menu presented a wonderful opportunity to gauge people's reactions to the English presence in the Ariège. It became a visual stimulus that I whipped out when talking to the incomers.

I had a good idea of what Gerald would say about the menu's illogical mixing of French and English. 'What comes to mind when you see that?' I said as I handed the photo across the tea table. He laughed. 'It's a bit of a mess, isn't it? Put it this way, we'd avoid that unless we were desperate.' I explained where it was and his tone became more serious. 'I know the one. That menu. We're never tempted to go in there. I mean, why would you come to France and eat bread pudding? Come to France and you can eat crème caramel.' Yet he went on to describe his own visit to the café. 'The owner was really short and rude. We never went in again.'

Fast-forward to a couple of years later when the café was taken over by an English woman who happened to be a friend of the couple. Gerald's wife promoted it enthusiastically on one of the Ariège forums as somewhere for the Brits to indulge in familiar treats such as Victoria sponge, English leaf teas and apple crumble with custard. As Sandra said, it was also a way to introduce the French to such delights, although it was *not meant to be an English tearoom*. Nevertheless, many Britons visiting the town saw it as a slice of England. Reading through its online reviews, I noted how the majority spoke positively about being able to find a full English breakfast among the medieval architecture, as well as the monthly visit of an English fish and chip van. I went out of my way to take a look. It was difficult to imagine how the menu would have met Gerald's approval, as it had retained its curious Franglais mix. If anything, it had become even more disorderly now it included *carrotte cake, sorbets of citron, myrtilles et mangue* and a *Full English breakfast – All Day!* The former French name had also been replaced by one in English: *The Mad Hatter*. I sat down and ordered in French, which the waitress dismissed with a wave of her hand: 'It's ok, I'm English.'

Back in Gerald's courtyard, I got up to go and mentioned the English-owned bed and breakfast that I'd booked myself into. Gerald immediately launched into a description of the owner and the recent dinner that they'd had together. He waved me off, standing outside his front door that opened directly onto the street. 'You'll be fine with Tony, he'll look after you.' As I made my way back to the car I wondered how long it would be before that longing for the hundred percent would pull Gerald and his wife back to England.

MURIEL'S ABOUT

'One of the things we decided right at the start was just total immersion. If it's a French system, we'll have that, thank you very much, and goodbye to the rest.' Pat and John's house sat in the centre of their village and our conversation was punctuated by the occasional sounds of traffic. At one point I jumped at the roar of next door's mower, starting up mere inches away on the other side of the fence.

Pat and John were exceptionally eager to chat with me, interrupting and talking over each other as they recounted everything about their move to this small village and what they got up to now they were here. They'd moved to the Ariège without knowing anything about it before the house purchase – "no history, no background, nothing" – and they'd even decided against the house on its first viewing. It was only a phone call from the estate agent – '"You do realise this ticked virtually every single box you'd got?"' quoted John – that drew them back for another look at it. They'd originally purchased it as a holiday home, but when John was offered early retirement they took the opportunity to make a permanent move, and they were now relieved that they'd chosen something small and manageable. 'If we'd originally set out looking for somewhere to live, I'd have been ridiculously tempted to buy a very large property with an enormous amount of land,' said John, 'but our friends over here already suffer with having houses that are miles too big and gardens that are unmanageable. We know quite a few who've had to downsize, both in land and in house.'

Pat nodded. 'Obviously you can get a lot for your money here, and people are thinking *Oh god, you get all that for that! So I'll have that*. But then they realise they can't manage the land, the habitation tax is quite high on bigger properties, there's the heating it and all the rest of it, and so they perhaps realise they've made a bit of an error.'

They'd both made a valiant effort to learn French, speaking with an accent coloured with a Midlands twang that I found familiar and comforting, although it brought some vowels closer to an English pronunciation. John talked about a week's holiday *down in the cruise* being a trigger point for them to think about buying in France. 'Department twenty-three, that,' added Pat. 'We'd originally wanted to live in the *Langwydoc*,' said Pat, 'but we couldn't find anything, and gradually moved further east to the *Ord* (Aude). But when the estate agent said *there's a house in the Ari-ayge*, we said, *Where's that?*'

The conversation came back again and again to how Pat and John weren't like the other Brits. Just as Gerald had distanced himself from the bread pudding eaters, Pat and John were similarly keen to show me that they weren't the kind of English incomers who were "really obsessed with buying English foods and things like that, which we find really sad." I thought back to my recent visits to nearby Mirepoix and the little groups of Brits I'd heard organising their get-togethers. The place had been described as *a magnet for the English* on the online forum, and it was close enough for me to have cycled there and back this morning after parking my car at their house. I wondered how Pat and John felt about having the "Dordogne phenomenon" on their doorstep and I brought out the photograph of the menu with its untidy Franglais. Pat was disdainful, recognising the café and remarking that a lot of people boycott it. 'I definitely wouldn't go to a place like that myself, because I feel as if it's not what I'm here for.'

John came in with a different reason. 'I'd ignore it on the basis that it's not a menu du jour or a plat du jour.'

'Yes,' said Pat, 'but we don't like the whole idea of having to have an English tearoom type of thing. We call this kind of thing *Muriel*, don't we?' she said, turning to John.

'*Muriel?*' I queried.

'Yes,' said Pat. 'We heard this once,' she said, and then put on a well-to-do voice: '*Oh Muriel, I've found an English tearoom over here, Muriel, come along*, and ever since then we say, O*h, Muriel's about.*'

It was true that most of the people I spoke to, when asked about a British community in the Ariège, cited Mirepoix as the place where one was most likely to be found. The town had had a British shop until recently, and Pat and John admitted to having visited it on a couple of occasions. According to Pat, this was only when they'd had English guests. 'We've just been to take visitors who just wanted to have a look or buy a bag of Walker's crisps.'

Out of everyone I spoke to, Pat and John lived the closest to this English magnet, and perhaps this was why they put so much effort into playing down the idea of living among large numbers of Brits. Going back to my earlier question about the English voices I'd heard, I asked if they knew where they all actually lived. John replied that there were "some in and around *Mirror-poix* and one or two in other villages around", making it sound inconsequential.

'We don't like it, do we,' added Pat. 'But this side, where we are, there's just three.' Instead they kept mentioning a village called Léran, where apparently most of the Brits were clustered – "over 60 English people living in Léran" – as well as many more British second home owners. The details became more sensational as they talked over each other, describing Léran as a place where there'd been "a little bit of unrest" in recent years, including a village murder. Pat filled me in. 'It sounds a bit like it was in the social housing type situation. I go to yoga there and one week the window had been smashed in the village hall. I've noticed how many *for sale* signs have been going up in Léran, because people have had enough now.' They mentioned one particular bar/restaurant run by English speakers that was the hub of the English activity. 'It centres around the bar and sometimes there's 20 people, it's sort of cliquey. The Brits all meet in the bar and they all get pissed.'

I later realised that this restaurant was the one most regularly mentioned on the online forum, being popular not only for its food but also the regular music nights. Unlike the Mirepoix café it kept its English and French menus separate, and it certainly wasn't aimed just at the Brits, although it did advertise afternoon tea. The incomers would also have appreciated the English book swaps that took place there. It had an adventurous and experimental menu – *Daube de boeuf a la Guinness* was a popular dish, as well as *Scotch eggs avec confit d'oignons* to start and *Bakewell tart* to finish off. I could see how it had become a go-to place for the English to meet up, without it being a strictly English restaurant. I took the opportunity to eat there one night, taking a seat in front of a bookcase filled with English books and picking up a copy of *Hello* magazine with the British royal family on the cover. But the place certainly wasn't bursting with English speakers that night, nor, after wandering around the village, did I feel any sense of being in a place overrun with social problems.

John began to bring in more evidence to show that if the Brits made a nuisance of themselves, it was always elsewhere. 'There was an incident in the pub by the bridge by Moulin

Neuf with one or two English that were getting overly drunk,' he said, referring to a nearby village.

Pat took up the story. 'And apparently they sat on someone's seat that was an old French guy's or something and it ended up in a fight.' The Brits clearly had a bit of a reputation in the area, which had made it necessary to steer the conversation away from their own backyard and focus on the issues elsewhere, in order to increase the physical distance between them and the drunken fights of the troublemakers. And at the other end of the social scale were the Muriels, portrayed as different people altogether, with their posh accents and penchant for English tearooms.

Despite all of this, English things continued to play a role. I'd noticed a British-registered 4×4 parked outside the house, yet irritation spilled out of John when he talked about the Brits who still drove a British-registered car. These were all placed into the category of annoying Brits who "don't really live here", together with the Brits who don't pay their French taxes. Lest I get the wrong idea, John went into a long explanation about why he himself still had a British vehicle plate, describing it as a non-option – "we don't have a choice, we can't have a French-registered car" – because his former place of work entitled them to a lease car, even during retirement. Due to this they drove back to England every few months to update the car. Moreover, they took the opportunity to fill it with the one food that they missed. 'We bring lots of bacon back, buying it in big bulk packs from a guy who runs a market stall that we've sort of got to know. We'll tell very close friends we're going to England and ask if they want anything.'

They also brought back British paint and teabags. John was a keen DIY-er who went into enthusiastic detail about how he'd put right the "horrendous wreck" of the house: he pointed out to me the exterior cladding, double glazing, new kitchen and electrics that he'd done. He also emphasised that the interior decoration had been done using British paint, as the French stuff was "akin to coloured water" as well as being much more expensive than the British brands. I was beginning to see that *total immersion* was open to interpretation.

One such interpretation related to John's idea that the English had a requirement, or duty, to share their culture with the French. This helped to justify the different British-themed food nights that they went to in some of the English-speaking restaurants around. Pat described a Welsh bar that started off doing Sunday lunches and moved into fish and chip shop nights, followed by St Patrick's nights and Robert Burns' nights. 'They were inundated. They had a big French following as well so that it was half French and half English. The French loved it and you don't mind so much then.'

John nodded. 'There was a lot of integration,' he said. 'You can't spin it the wrong way. There's an expectation in the minds of the average French person. A large part of them want to understand culturally where you are. So I think there's a requirement on us to share that culture with the French, in the same way as we want to share theirs.' I nodded slowly as I tried to get my head around this idea of a French expectation.

Pat expanded on the idea of sharing. 'It's as if you're bringing something, a bit quirky perhaps, to their village. And they're curious and they're sort of integrated.'

I could see the point about the quirkiness, and it was an ingenious argument to dispel any contradiction with what they'd said earlier about finding those who obsessed over English food as "really sad". They saw themselves as participating in an important exchange, just doing their duty to address a French expectation. In this way it was presented as part of the French way of life. *You can't spin it the wrong way.*

I could imagine the French viewing their English quirkiness with genuine affection.

But both Pat and John had mentioned *integration* as if it was the French who were "sort of integrated". Of course integration is a two-way street, where the host is as responsible for accepting the incomers and their quirks as the incomers are responsible for not segregating themselves. Yet the language that they used went beyond the idea of French acceptance, suggesting a degree of responsibility with the French themselves to become integrated into the English social activities. It was an idea that had been raised in some academic circles, that a degree of local adaptation to the culture of immigrants was a good thing, although it was a controversial idea too.

Today it was an idea that was helping to diminish the responsibility to avoid everything English. It was their way of making it clear to me that they were doing the right thing. After all, they were simply meeting the needs and curiosity of the French, who really do want to understand these quirky English people who have come to live in their town. Not like those stuck-up Muriels.

GUESTS OF HONOUR

'Is any of this any good to you?' demanded John as we sat around drinking yet more tea. I nodded, feeling an undercurrent of delight that they were so eager to provide me with detailed accounts of their social life.

'I know we do talk too much,' said Pat. I reassured them that this wasn't the case and asked them what came to mind with the words *British community in Ariège*. I was interested to see how they would avoid reference to nearby magnet-for-the-English Mirepoix. 'Well, Léran would spring to mind immediately,' said Pat. 'I don't think there's one here, but we've seen it in Léran.'

John came in to water down the idea. 'But hang on, it's not Dordogne, so the answer is no, there isn't a British community here. There are pockets, that's all.'

Pat persisted. 'If you spoke to Hannah, the other English person in our village, she would tell you exactly the opposite. She goes to the Women's Group, she goes to the English service in Mirepoix cathedral, they've let them have it there, and there are spin-off church groups, all English. She goes to the book group, and a discussion group; the topics might be anything from euthanasia to gardening in France, but it's all done in English. It's all English speakers who go to it.'

John's insistence that just a few Brits were living in the area was rapidly evaporating. 'In that case, yes, there are lots of things that the English do,' he conceded, 'but it's not Dordogne, it is the Ariège, and I guess there's a thin scattering that tend to permeate towards an organised centre. But then it peters out.'

So there were more English incomers and organised social activities than they'd originally implied, but it was also true that Mirepoix was only a shadow of the clichéd little England of the Dordogne, with its Gentlemen's and Ladies' clubs as well as cricket clubs. Nor was it like the Brit-populated Aquitaine, where there were associations for veterans of the RAF and the Royal Navy. According to the anthropologist Kate Fox, this ritual of setting up clubs wherever we go reflects more about the social inadequacies of the English as a race than any practical needs; the argument is that we need clubs as a prop to overcome our generally poor ability to engage socially. The English-speaking clubs and groups in and around Mirepoix would certainly provide a means of socialising in a comfortable environment. While each club had a specific named function that was outwardly its sole purpose, they would also have provided a less visible social networking opportunity for the English-speaking incomers, particularly those with less-than-adequate skills in French. Yet I was wary of generalising à la Fox, and Pat went on to describe less formal gatherings, such as a discussion group that took place between the English-speaking incomers and French locals who were keen to improve their English. The group met regularly and took away homework to prepare for the next discussion, which might be on topics related to French literature and radio programmes. This clearly had a practical purpose in improving language skills, but it would also provide a less threatening environment for socialising with the French, who were also working on language skills. Everyone was there to improve in one way or another.

The conversation shifted to the kinds of activities they did, with a focus on the amount of fun that they had because they made an effort to go to every social occasion in the village. At the same time, the moralistic undertones conveyed that they were doing things the right way. 'We make an effort so that we're shown to be taking full advantage of the French way of life and not sort of isolating ourselves, which I'd hate to do,' added Pat. And apparently the French took notice of this and showed their approval; making an effort to go and vote in the local elections had earned them "a round of applause".

At one point I jumped as the lawnmower started up again – "that's Bernard mowing his lawn" – which was an opportunity to bring in an anecdote about being invited to his daughter's wedding where, according to Pat, they were treated "like royalty" simply for being British. 'Like guests of honour,' agreed John. '*Have a photograph taken with the English.*'

'Yeah, it was like we were these freaks,' added Pat. 'It was nice because you feel like you are properly being integrated, which is important.' But to me this conveyed a sense of standing out rather than a sense of integration – as if they were members of an exotic tribe, to be photographed with. Being made to feel like guests of honour, or royalty, conveyed a sense of importance, of celebrity even, simply due to being from England. It also suggested a kind of hierarchy – *we're part of the community, but our Englishness puts us on a different level.* The English have a reputation for patronising foreigners for their funny ways, and perhaps this was an example: *the French are so funny, making us feel special like this!* It had been the same at an international rugby match televised in the village hall. 'They kept giving us free food and beers because we were like the celebrity guests again,' said Pat. 'It was quite funny.'

But the word *freaks* implied something else, and it wasn't an image that many would aspire to. It certainly didn't sit easily with Pat's claim that it showed they were *properly being integrated;* if anything, it implied that they stood out and were treated as something abnormal. Maybe the French appreciated their efforts and found their accent rather charming? I was no stranger to standing out due to a Midlands accent; during my first year at university, my insufferably snobbish public school peers would introduce me to their friends, and then – "Listen to this!" – they'd ask me to "say the word *bucket*". I suppose it was better than being a Muriel.

A year or so later I gave a talk on this bizarre use of "freaks" and "royalty" at a linguistics conference, where a well-known scholar of the language of tourism was in the audience. During the question session he became animated, objecting to my description of Pat and John as "migrants". 'These aren't migrants! They're tourists!' he shrieked. 'They have the privilege of being able to go home at any time!' He also found their use of the word *freaks* bordering on the offensive: it's fun to be a freak, when you can easily retreat to a safe place.

I didn't wholly agree with what he was saying. The French, with their invitations and requests for photographs, provided a form of self-gratification for the English couple. Pat and John must have been aware that they could never sink invisibly into French society, but they would have been dismayed if the French had simply ignored all this effort. Some appreciation was necessary, and even being feted as abnormal in some way was evidence that they were being noticed. It would be vastly preferable to receiving the cold shoulder. Like Gerald, they saw the positives in being cultural outsiders, although they interpreted it as an environment of celebrity rather than the freedom to be eccentric and make mistakes.

All of this socialising needed at least a basic level of French language, and Pat had a head start from her long-ago schooldays. John had invested time in language classes before they made the move, and unlike Gerald, for whom being good wasn't good enough, John showed no frustration and seemed content with his level of basic French. He put this down to being realistic in what was achievable, describing how he built up his vocabulary gradually around his interests of DIY and gardening. 'I just learn it on a need-to-know basis,' he said. 'That's what they call a saw, that's what they call a lawnmower.' But pronunciation was a different matter, and like everyone else they described the Ariège accent as impenetrable at times. Their own Midlands-infused pronunciation must have caused the odd difficulty too. They recounted a tale of a Toulouse shopkeeper not understanding their pronunciation of *pain au raisins,* and while Pat admitted that she'd probably not got the pronunciation quite right, John shifted the blame to the shopkeeper's intellect. 'We'd have got more sense out of that wall,' he said, gesturing towards the edge of the courtyard.

I asked about their use of the online forums and Pat described how she liked to help where she could, admitting that she also found them interesting to read. I asked what I thought was a fairly neutral question. 'Can you tell much about people from what they write on the forum?'

'Absolutely,' jumped in John. 'Idiots jumping out off the page.'

Pat nodded. 'Some of them, you think, please don't come and live in France.'

John was even blunter. 'Most of them I look at and say, please go home. They go on about inane things, which simply explain that they don't understand the French system and they don't have the savvy to go out and get what they need.'

Pat admitted feeling sorry for some of the new arrivals. 'Those who really haven't got a clue and I don't know whether they'll last. They're going to be looking for work but there's a lot of unemployment here and you're going to be at the bottom of the list.' Her tone became more scornful. 'People thinking they can come and run a gîte or a bar, all this sort of *dreamland*.'

John put it down to basic economics. 'There's an awful lot of books written about living in France but not one that I've read sets out the real basics about income versus expenditure. Someone needs to be a bit more protective towards some of the souls that plan on coming over.'

He was also scathing about people who chose this part of France for the weather. 'If you come with a view that you're actually just moving for the climate, then forget it, because you don't get the climate without the culture. It's the culture that, for me, drives the French way of life. The importance of food, the importance of family.'

As the weeks went on I heard others talk about the importance of family here in France. Hardly anyone acknowledged how it contradicted their decision to move away from their own family members back in the UK, although almost everyone talked about someone they knew going back because they were too far away from family. According to Pat, the other English person in their village, a single female, had planned to return, since she missed spending time with her daughter.

'That's all gone on the back burner now she's got a dog,' said Pat. 'She's not selling her house anymore. But there's a lot of women who live on their own here, women who perhaps think, *oh, you know, perhaps I should be there for them*, say if their daughter's ill, or the grandchildren.'

It was an ethical dilemma for many, but Pat and John were adamant that they had the solution. 'I do genuinely feel I'm missing out with the grandchildren, but if they come here and spend a holiday with us, you're with them 24/7. That's more like quality time than if I was rushing from house to house back in England,' said Pat. 'But I don't feel guilty about it 'cause I've done my bit in life, I've had kids. I've worked hard.'

John jumped in to reinforce the logic of their way of thinking. 'It *is* a difficult balance and you can interpret it as selfishness or you can interpret it on the basis that *I've done my bit, I've done 42 years, I've done on average 50–60 hours a week, and by the way, I just reckon I deserve a bit of time as well*. But there are people with a completely different view that will exclusively fixate around the family and the children. Well, they can carry on, but don't criticise or don't believe that there isn't another way.' Each to his own, then.

As the conversation drew to a close, John added a point that must have been developing in his mind over the course of the afternoon, something about exactly why they were living in France. 'The biggest thing that France presents for me on a daily basis is a challenge. It's something I've got to get to grips with and work at. A lot of people don't get to enjoy their retirement because they become introverted and they just disappear. Being here gives me something to focus on and work at.' It was a sentiment that I was to hear often over the next few weeks, as an important push factor for the move among people close to retirement. The right house, a slower pace of life, the climate and the uncrowdedness were all pull factors that drew people to France, but some incomers were set on escaping not just England itself, but an uneventful and predictable way of life that stretched into the horizon.

Life in the Ariège was summed up by Pat as one that offered people more freedom. She compared it with England. 'There it seems to be rules, rules, rules, rules, rules. Here you can just go for a swim in the lake and that's lovely, it's much more a sort of laid-back, hippy lifestyle.' It was true that there were no rules against swimming in some of the mountain lakes, the étangs, and many a time I'd toiled uphill for two to three hours, to find the clear water gently rippled by a swimmer doing breaststroke. But not all of the lakes allowed swimming.

I thanked them and stood up to go, casually mentioning that I'd be calling into the nearby DIY centre. John's eyes lit up. 'What are you going to buy?' I replied that I was just going to get a replacement tin of paint, expecting him to shake his head at the idea of French paint. He asked what the brand was and then nodded his approval. 'Yes, that's the best one out here. It's the only French brand worth buying.' I felt that I'd gone up in his estimation now, showing my colours as a true Brit DIYer and, moreover, able to tell good paint from bad. 'It's a good place, the Brico centre,' he nodded. 'We go down there pretty much every day.'

A MORE HUMAN SORT OF ACCEPTANCE

Pleased that I'd managed to find the right shade of *eau de nil*, I left the Brico centre and headed for a hamlet that was not even marked on my map. The approach roads were barely discernible on paper, but I did notice that there was a *voie verte* – a traffic-free greenway for cyclists – that passed close to their hamlet. I was glad that I still had the bike in the car, feeling more confident negotiating the narrow roads on two wheels rather than four. Arriving by bike turned out to be a good strategy for breaking the ice during that late summer wave of heat that was increasing in its ferocity. People were expecting something else – a car and clipboard? – rather than a red-faced perspiring cyclist, and once they'd got over their surprise, they invariably sat me down in the shade and rushed away to fetch me a cold drink, perhaps worried that I was going to succumb to a heart attack or a stroke in their garden.

Like almost every other English incomer I spoke to, Gail and Mike were welcoming and spoke effusively about their life in the foothills of the Pyrenees. Mike knew the general area from when he'd studied in France in his youth, and they'd looked for a house that was within driving distance of the sea as well as the mountains. Aged in their 40s, Gail and Mike were renovating an enormous country house that in the past had been the home to over thirty families who laboured in a nearby factory. The factory itself lay derelict close by. For the meantime the couple were concentrating on getting just half of the house habitable. Mike also did odd-jobbing as a builder, which put him in demand with the English incomers who wanted to be sure of what they were getting in their renovations.

Their garden was as large as a small park, crowned at one end by the forested foothills of the Pyrenees, and by the enormous house in its half-and-half state at the other. It was difficult to drag my eyes away from the gaping hole in the roof of the untouched section. We sat around a table while Gail served tea and talked about the kind of life they had here in the Ariège countryside.

'I shop at Aldi and Lidl, which I'd never have done in England, not because we're poor or on a budget, but because we don't live like we did in England.'

'That's living like the French do,' said Mike. 'We're not consumerist like we would have been in England.'

'They just don't do the consumerism thing here. We've completely changed in that respect.' This didn't mean that they lived rustically. I felt scruffy and damp sitting next to elegant Gail and a later tour of the good half of the house revealed a stylish French *eau de nil* colour scheme that made me realise that my own DIY attempts hadn't *quite* got it right.

Nor did it mean that France was a cheaper place to live. During the 19th century, Britons had made their way to France for a less expensive way of life, and they'd continued to do so even when the comparative cost of living was no longer lower than in Britain. France had been a place where the English upper classes could live more economically, with fewer or no servants and less expensive entertaining, in a way that might cause an embarrassing loss of face back in England. There were still some parallels to be seen in the current day influxes, and one of these was the purchase of a home. Certainly the English were finding that their money went further in the Ariège, even if they'd originally wanted to live further east. Mike and Gail's purchase of a mansion was an extreme example of this. And although there was less pressure nowadays to adhere to the expectations of one's social class, the less commercialised Ariège made it easier to resist the relentless temptations of consumerism.

Mike was a competent French speaker, which led Gail, who had missed out on learning the language at school, to rely on him. 'I mostly pick it up and I know a lot but I'm not good enough at putting it together quick enough to say something.' I asked if this made her feel like an outsider at times. 'Maybe just with the language frustration, and then I think, oh God, they could be thinking *stupid English woman*.' It was the complete opposite to John's idea that a miscommunication might be down to the French not being clever enough to understand them. Over the next few weeks I began to notice how common it was for females to talk about themselves rather negatively when they saw themselves from a French perspective. Elaine, whose French was basic, explained how she tried to make sure that the French didn't dismiss her as '*just that silly English woman who's an immigrant. And why's she here? She can't even speak our language*, you know.' But such feelings weren't confined to those with limited French. Rosie, a French speaker, also sensed the negative gaze of the locals: 'as soon as anyone slightly doesn't like me because I'm a foreigner or something, then I start stammering and stuttering all over the place, which is crazy.' It wasn't just the language-related limitations in dealing with returning faulty shop items or querying a telecoms bill. Feeling like an outsider could make an incomer feel foolish, particularly when they imagined themselves seen through the eyes of the French.

It's easy to underestimate the importance of language when caught up with the excitement of finding a wonderful house in which to spend the rest of your days, especially when the property magazines and television programmes focus on getting the most for your money at the expense of more practical day-to-day issues. Newcomers on the Ariège forum talked about learning French as if it was a simple case of opening one's mouth and being fed the language. And for those who'd read Peter Mayle, it was probably reassuring that his narrative began with "an almost total lack of comprehension" during their first dinner with neighbours at the start of the Provençal year, but by the autumn appeared to have progressed to an ability to make complicated phone calls. Gail was an example of how it really wasn't that simple, having given up on a beginner's Open University course that was pitched more at intermediates. She was now relying on the radio and language tapes to improve, whilst Mike was left to sort out situations.

I asked about the English people that they knew. Gail remarked how they didn't really know people of their own age, being in between the younger families who were moving out and those of retirement age. 'I tend not to enjoy the company of English people when I'm in France,' Mike added, although it was noticeable that they avoided the rants and clichés about the "other" Brits that I'd been hearing up till now. Mike admitted that he'd come across some who seemed unprepared, but it was a refreshing change to hear incomers described more in terms of personality, rather than the clichés of nationality. Mike described "the sort of people who just go, like, *here we go, life experience*, and blunder through life, unaware of the chaos". And rather than mindlessly repeating the mantra to speak French and integrate, Mike became pragmatic and honest when he acknowledged that different versions of the dream existed. For some it could mean living in the mountains and having "absolutely nothing to do with anybody, French or English".

It was quite a contrast to Pat and John's insistence on being seen to "take advantage" of every opportunity to socialise because they were afraid of how the French might categorise them. Mike's vision was more about being accepted for what you are, rather than whether you did or didn't fit into the national stereotype. 'It's more about how you are… it's a more human sort of acceptance; the country doesn't really have any relevance.' It certainly made sense when considering the people living quietly in the higher Pyrenees, who were often French themselves.

Out came the photo of the café menu. Mike laughed. 'That menu says to me *I'm not going in there.*'

Gail nodded. 'Mike wouldn't want to go in there, but I'm a foodie so I'll try anything. But from an aesthetic point of view, it's a mess.'

Mike zoomed in on the language. 'Why translate tuna and not *jambon*? It's unnatural, isn't it? Strange.' What was also surprising was that they both knew enough about the place to comment on the staff serving there, despite Mike's insistence that he would avoid it at all cost.

As I switched off my recorder I asked if they had any questions. 'Would you like another cup of tea?' asked Mike.

'And a tour of the house,' added Gail. An hour later I got back on the bike feeling like I'd spent an afternoon with friends, and I rode away with an invitation to return for dinner some time.

COQ AU VIN À DEUX

Back at the car, I peeled off my cycling shorts and used them as a barrier against the unbearably hot steering wheel as I headed for that night's accommodation. Naturally, I'd looked for an English-run B&B where I might continue my observations. It turned out that Tony was running the place solo, as his wife Debbie was on a visit to the UK. As with Gerald's wife, it was a visit that she would prefer to be permanent, and because of that, the guest house was up for sale. It was too much of a tie, one that negatively affected their social life. Moreover, Debbie missed their daughter, who'd stayed behind in England when the couple had decided to move to the Ariège.

Although I'd been told that evening meals were not provided, Tony immediately asked me if I would like to eat with him, since there were no restaurants around and he had nothing else to do. It was all very casual; when I went to pay the following morning, he merely shrugged his shoulders when I asked how much extra for the coq au vin. I had to estimate what I thought was a fair price. I sensed that Tony was a bit lonely, and as the sole guest I sat through a detailed description of his former life in England, where he had earned lots of money but had been permanently stressed. He gestured his hand towards the deserted road beyond the kitchen window: 'This is our rush hour.' But he went on to describe their Ariège summers as one long frenzied treadmill, when they were "too busy with guests to even make a cup of tea." His main complaint was that guests wouldn't leave them alone, yet here he was following me around and even setting the breakfast table for two so that he could sit opposite me and continue to provide what he called "fodder" for my research. Despite the non-stop whirl of the summer season, its shortness meant that they "didn't make much" from the business, and most of the off-season was spent doing odd jobs for the local Brits, such as painting shutters and organising holiday home changeovers. Even this off-season fill-in work was described as a never-ending race from property to property, one that took up all of his time so that he never even got to use the season's ski pass he'd invested in. He made it sound as if the Brits needed their shutters painting every single year.

I asked Tony if he socialised with other English people, but he claimed not to; he was especially keen to shun British social gatherings in what he called "a pub-type setting". Yet he lived in a hamlet where half a dozen other English incomers were living, and it sounded as if he mixed with them. He also knew many of the other incomers with whom I was meeting up, even those from much further afield, partly because they'd hosted lunches for the Ariège English Speaking Women's Group. The tales of his former life and the British gossip might have carried on until the early hours if I hadn't made my excuses and left.

When I asked Tony for his thoughts on why people might be moving to the Ariège, he was adamant that the Dutch were the most obvious and numerous incomers. The Dutch, he stated, were completely taking over certain villages – "far more than the English do" – driving down with their cars stuffed full of Dutch food and contributing nothing locally, in his view. It was apparently all down to the relative height of the Ariège above sea level. The Dutch were naturally alarmed at the prospect of further sea level rises as the Earth continued to warm up, and the Ariège had been noted as somewhere where sustainable living would be possible in the event of environmental collapse. 'It's high, it's south and it's wooded. People are moving here with their children's futures in mind.'

It wasn't just something that individuals were considering for themselves. Flying back to the Ariège from the UK recently, Tony had got talking to some people who were taking the interest in self-sufficiency even further, as a business opportunity. They told him that they were coming to the Ariège with the aim of looking to buy an entire hamlet, in order to set up an eco-business, bringing in people to teach others how to live a self-sufficient life. 'Were they like the alternative types around here?' I asked.

'No,' said Tony. 'They were business people. They were honest in admitting that they weren't particularly alternative themselves. They just saw it as an opportunity to make money out of those who were. There are people out there who are worried enough to want to escape but they don't know how to go about it.' So it was a kind of free-market exploitation, of people and their fears, and of the Ariège landscape too. Perhaps it would work, but the underlying capitalist motivation seemed to jar with what they proclaimed to be promoting. There were plenty of opportunities around for volunteers to join eco-projects where they would help with various tasks such as market gardening and dry stone walling, and at the same time develop their own knowledge of sustainable living. I'd picked up hitchhiking student architects who were volunteering at one such eco-enterprise near Massat; they were learning about traditional roofing and they received free accommodation in return for their labour. But there was no exchange of money.

Seeing the Ariège as a way to exploit people's anxieties about the future seemed an undesirable concept, but why? It's a packaging and marketing of the land in a way that's capitalising on people's desire to live a simpler life, but was it really that different from the way that some estate agents sell property with an accompanying concept of a way of life, filling the property magazines or the exhibition halls in London with glossy images to entice buyers to purchase a lifestyle? Perhaps it was. A fair portion of the Ariège was up for sale to individuals enticed by the glorious isolation of a converted barn far from any other habitation, but the incomers would need to adapt to the land; taming it into submission as necessary, but also adapting their way of life to whatever the land inflicted on them. But this purchase of an entire village to exploit a gap in the market seemed to be the other way round. Here were business-minded incomers imposing a way of life on the land where the original knowledge was long gone. The buyers would bring in others to reinvent something that was similar but superficial, designed for profit, rather than something they really believed was the right thing to do. It felt like an unwelcome exploitation of the wild and free Ariège and it made me uneasy.

2

WE DID IT ALL WRONG

SOMETIMES I THINK I SHOULD
HAVE MOVED TO CUMBRIA

'I don't rave about France itself. I like this area for what it is, but if it gets too overpopulated then I would go. Sometimes I think I should have just moved up north, it wouldn't be very much different than if I'd moved to Cumbria.' Tina and I were behind the counter in a shop in a small Ariège town, surrounded by English food items for sale: baked beans, ketchup, custard and mustard. There was also a wall shelved with used English language paperbacks, available to buy for a couple of euros. Tina, perched on the counter in her jeans, jumped up every now and then to serve the people coming into the shop: the odd English incomer wanting a chat, a few French customers buying teabags and an American woman who lived nearby and was down on her luck. She would have talked at us for the entire afternoon if Tina hadn't made a gentle hint.

Tina admitted that the decision to move here had been totally spur of the moment. They'd taken a wrong turn whilst on holiday, and had ended up buying a holiday home after casually looking in an estate agent's window. It didn't take long for them to decide to leave England behind for good, although at times it sounded as if they'd swapped their English stress for an Ariège version. 'I had a career and a nice job and a nice house and lots of money and then you come here and it's completely different. I suppose, if you like, I ran away.' Despite an early claim that "we wouldn't go back now", Tina steered the conversation through numerous disappointments and pitfalls, all of which were painstakingly detailed. If any visitors had come into the shop with the idea of moving here, as they often did, they would probably have left the shop shaking their head and feeling relieved to have had a lucky escape.

Although Tina went on to mention what she called the "Peter Mayle factor", she began by articulating the push factors for the move much more strongly than the pull of France itself. Demanding jobs, stress-related illness and the process of "becoming your own person" after divorce were all given as factors that drove the couple to start living permanently over here, despite Tina's nine-year-old daughter choosing to stay behind at the last minute. 'To be honest I thought it'd be much easier to pop back, but it's not just popping back. Flights not running in the winter, two hours to the airport, you know, and you can't just take time off work so I don't see her as much as I'd like.' On the other hand, Tina acknowledged that the area wasn't ideal for an English teenager. 'In hindsight, for her, definitely I wouldn't have brought her here.'

The couple had initially struggled to find work in the Ariège, with Tina doing odd cleaning jobs for other English-speaking incomers until she'd recently been taken on to run the shop full time. Despite the obvious enjoyment she got from the job, and from her relationship with the owner – "she's like our family now" – Tina radiated disappointment rather than smugness about the new life. 'I don't like it when the English come over here and say how fantastic it is compared to England, because I don't think it is when you work here.' She also exuded anxiety about the approaching winter. Having lived through four Ariège winters, she talked about getting really depressed at night because of the impending end of summer. 'I haven't worked in the winter yet but I don't think it's going to be much fun. I think January's going to be very quiet here, but also getting home at half six, seven o'clock at night is going to be quite depressing.'

It illustrated the difference between the imagined life and reality. The cliché of the rural idyll had been a pull for Tina, who referred to it as the "Peter Mayle factor" within "that little French dream". 'We're not pottering up and walking around the market with your wicker basket and all that,' she laughed. 'I bought the basket and everything, but I'm never there on market days as I'm working. One of the first things we did was get bikes because it's the whole *A Year in Provence* thing, isn't it, that we're going to do. We go mushroom picking every year just so that we can go and make idiots of ourselves at the chemist. I remember getting that from Peter Mayle's book, but you go to the chemist and they go *Non, non, non*. I've never picked a good mushroom yet.'

Living in Ariège wasn't entirely a disappointment. For Tina, life here was still relaxed compared with the way things had been in England. 'I completely lived off stress. Completely and utterly. It was 14-hour days, you know, to the childminder's, 8 o'clock in the morning, pick up 7 o'clock at night, go go go,' she rattled off. 'I had to have medication so I could actually go to sleep because you couldn't switch off.' But as the afternoon drew on, she became ever less enthusiastic in her descriptions of Ariège life, sharing her irritations about absolutely everything but in a fairly good-natured way. I guessed that she probably enjoyed having a moan to a sympathetic stranger in order to balance out the hours spent with the eager customers who came in to ask her advice about moving here.

I brought up the questions brought up by newcomers on the forum and received a hollow laugh. 'They're so enthusiastic and so excited about it and on a high, you know, it's all so fantastic.' But according to Tina, what they would find when they got here was that the social charges were horrendous, the tax system was a minefield and a so-called fantastic health cover system that 'horrified' her. The latter was given as the ultimate reason for the return of no less than three retired couples to the UK. Everyday living was made difficult by the price of electricity, petrol, meat and road tolls, and there were no affordable clothes shops in the town. The local weather wasn't acquitted either; according to Tina it rained every day in July but it was really, really hot in August, when you just want it to rain. Even "going to the doctors is quite hard, you just think, oh, can't be bothered". It all made me wonder why there wasn't a mass exodus of people leaving the country, including the French.

Like most of the other English incomers I met, Tina set herself apart from the other incomers, although she saw them less in terms of the stereotypes, and more as falling into one of two camps: the wealthier, older Brits and the younger alternative families. She seemed keen to avoid coming across within either category, describing herself as between the two. She described being invited for pre-dinner drinks and sitting looking over the pool of the wealthier incomers, whilst feeling a world apart. 'We're younger, got no pensions, no property in England, nothing like that.' Yet this was also cited as a positive factor in that it helped them to integrate. 'So many of the others don't have to work and they stay within their little community, so they aren't accepted like we are.' Apparently even the French had assumed that they were wealthy early-retirees, and Tina felt that they'd had to work really hard at dispelling that initial assumption among the locals. They'd done this, she said, by visiting the local bar every night to explain how they'd come to work, that they hadn't come with money to live on.

At the other end of the lifestyle-and-wealth spectrum were people that Tina felt were "like us but quite alternative". She'd been invited to music evenings and vegan barbeques, where Steiner school children ran around the "wooden shack" that was their home, one without television or washing machine and having only a compost toilet. 'Lovely if you can do it, but I can't,' she laughed. 'I don't dislike them and I've been to one or two gatherings and just thought, *I really just don't feel like I should be here.* You have a glass of wine and you're sort of looked at... they don't normally drink, they're just on the wacky, so yes, I think we're sort of not quite the norm here, if you like.' Even socialising after work with the local French was not the same as going out with English friends back in England. 'I think it can be quite lonely sometimes.'

Language learning doesn't come easy to everyone, and Tina felt she moved "backwards" when she first came to live here. As with many others, it was a case of bringing back to life the French learned some twenty, thirty or forty years ago in school. Apart from the discussion group used by Pat and John, I heard of only one formal opportunity to learn the language, some laughably poor classes that had taken place in Saint-Girons. Almost everyone I spoke to had attended them, but they all found it ludicrous that one teacher had to cope with a class of 30 odd people of different levels and nationalities – English, Dutch, Tahitian and Indian, to list a few. The English apparently nicknamed it "The Comedy Club" before they all gave it up as a waste of time.

The village of Léran had been on my mind since talking to Pat and John, and I wondered if Tina knew much about it. 'I heard there are a large number of English people in a place called Léran?' I asked.

Tina became animated, nodding. 'Yes, massive, huge, huge.'

'About 60 English people, so I was told?'

'Is it north, south of Carcassonne?' she asked.

'It's west,' I replied, wondering whether it had just been an automatic reaction to agree with me. Nothing more was offered and Tina moved on to what was going on in the neighbouring Aude département, in which she was an expert. She brought in an English character known as Little Fat Norman, who operates a business out of the neighbouring Aude département. I must have sounded sceptical that anyone would choose to operate under such a name, as Tina insisted on bringing up his website to prove the existence of the business.

'It's basically in an English village... there's quite a history around there with the English and obviously next to Carcassonne it's perfect for them. He buys in English food and sells it on to shops around the area.' Tina bent over her laptop, picking out what she thought I'd be interested in. 'He's got a poppy fair going on, look, two Chelsea pensioners are going. There's a monthly book exchange for the Brits, it's huge. There you go, Cornwall clotted cream tea... scones and jam. Oh, and a link to *Mr Sausage*, he's quite an interesting man, he makes his own English sausages.'

This was more like the British stereotype that I'd been hearing about. I looked up the website and it continues to advertise a surprising number of English food shops dotted around the Aude and further east, stocking quintessential *British grocery products,* many of which I'd have thought have perfectly good French versions, such as jam and marmalade. The website also offers a platform for English incomers to advertise their services: joiners, English television installation and will-making as well as English-speaking cancer support. It all looked more lively than anything I'd seen in the Ariège, but there again, the Aude département has a more sizeable population of Brits, whereas those in Ariège could never sustain such enterprises.

Tina was knowledgeable about the food supply process. 'People drive down with the goods, and if you're a seller then you have to price it at a certain rate. If you ever drive down here you could get paid to bring certain goods.' She seemed to be offering this as a suggestion to me, but I shook my head at the idea. It reminded me of when I drove on the ferry to come down here, staring into the Land Rover in front that was rammed full of toilet paper, about a year's supply for an average family. I'd wondered why on Earth anyone would need to bring a 4×4 load to France when the country was able to cope perfectly well with supply and demand.

I also thought about Pat and John and their car-loads of bacon, and wondered whether there was something that they hadn't told me.

WELCOME TO VALLEY COTTAGE

It was ten months since I'd last talked to Lynn. On a hot October afternoon we'd sat in white deckchairs emboldened with a red St George's cross, shouting above the noise of a concrete mixer as her partner Steve prepared the foundation platform of their building plot. Back then Lynn had been enthusiastic about the "absolutely beautiful Ariège" and optimistic about her forthcoming job interview for a professional healthcare position.

Now it was the following August. Cycling past the house, I'd been pleased to catch sight of Lynn in the garden and soon she was offering to show me around the completed interior of the house. Outside, the shiny slate roof was in place, although the

:k walls were starkly awaiting their final rendering.
drawn to spray-painted graffiti that shouted out
.velcome you to Valley Cottage around the front
, as well as *Max is the king!* sprayed onto the wall facing the
road. I also noticed a black metal nameplate bearing the English
house name. The St George's deckchairs were still there, placed
next to a small inflatable plunge pool. Steve said a quick hello
before turning to shout in slow and careful English to a man
leaning out of his car window on the road above. They appeared
to be arranging a time to go and work. 'He's a builder moved
down here from Paris,' said Lynn. 'Steve helps him out now and
then.' I was glad to hear that they'd both found employment.
But the house was already up for sale.

It turned out that Lynn had jumped the gun in
recommending the "quality of life" here before the concrete
of the house foundations had even set. I said I was sorry to
hear they were packing up so soon, but that they'd probably
had some fun along the way. 'No,' said Lynn, shaking her
head, 'we haven't enjoyed the experience at all. We have hardly
any time off and we rarely go anywhere. And I miss English
culture.' I turned to Steve, hoping for something more positive,
but he looked gloomy.

'Well, it's different here, isn't it – everything shuts down
between 12 and 2, you can't do anything.' It sounded an
underwhelming reason to move back to England, but the
notorious French bureaucracy had also played a part in making
them fed up with life in France. Lynn seemed worn out by the
different processes that were notorious for their complexity,
such as claiming back for doctor's bills and registering their
cars. Even being in the unusual and enviable position of having
a professional job hadn't helped.

'I thought having done some French at school and going to
classes for two years before we came would be ok,' she said,

but from the very first day in a healthcare job, Lynn had felt badly overwhelmed by the fast pace and the lack of support from colleagues. Moving down to a more junior role, she now found it easier to cope but it was frustrating, since she was over-qualified. They had had enough and were looking forward to moving back to the English Midlands.

The previous year she'd been aware that it wouldn't be a totally smooth ride but she'd spoken positively about being prepared to ride the waves. 'I know there are going to be some downs and you've got to be fairly strong. You know, I did question whether I was doing the right thing last year because we were out the end of July, and the 3 weeks we were here we had 6 lovely days, and the rest it rained and it rained, torrential rain, and I was gutted because we were moving from somewhere where it rains every day.' She pulled a face. 'It was a case of *oh my God, what am I coming to?* Plus there's not an awful lot around, and when it's miserable, it's bloody miserable.'

Ten months later it was clear that the trials of building a large house whilst living in a frozen-up caravan over an exceptionally harsh Pyrenean winter had ground them down to a point of no return. They'd rented a caravan on a nearby campsite, but as the temperatures dropped to below minus 20, they'd been left to cope with no water or flushing toilet, and nowhere to empty the bucket, for 56 days. At some point, without water access, Steve drank from the river in desperation, despite Lynn's warning about cows on the opposite bank, and he contracted dysentery. But for Lynn the "worst ever day" was when 120 sheets of plasterboard arrived in the snow and had to be carried down the steep drive to the house. In the end they'd made a sledge out of pallets and rope, working until night time to get the plasterboard indoors.

'We came here for the weather,' she said. 'We did it all wrong.'

Rewinding back to the previous October, my meeting with Lynn had been a kind of deliberately-by-chance meeting. I'd been cycling along one of the wider and sunnier river valleys coming down from the high ground, pedalling through a small village that had little sign of life – there was a small café dominated by the towering church nearby, but the tables were all empty. As the road began to rise my eye was caught by a building plot with two unmistakeably English deckchairs; the red St George's crosses on their white background stood out sharply against the grey concrete platform. I stopped and peered over the edge of the road, noticing a British-registered car parked alongside the plot. There didn't seem to be anyone about, but asking around, I found out that the builders were a newly arrived English couple. Intrigued by the symbolic deckchairs, I planned another bike ride past the site, and bingo, there they were, working on the house foundations. Lynn seemed pleased to stop work and chat about their project, pulling the deckchairs away so that we could hear each other over the grind of the concrete mixer.

Like Pat and John, Lynn and Steve had been introduced to this corner of France by an estate agent. 'We didn't really know France very well to be honest. It wasn't a case that we'd had regular visits over here; it was really because I spoke French a little from school and France isn't a million miles away from England, which is important because we've got adult children back in England.' It was an unusual case of language being the deciding factor without much knowledge of the actual country, although they were aware of the clichés associated with the Brits in France. 'We wanted to go and engage in French culture, so we knew we didn't want to go to the Dordogne. We wanted the weather, and somewhere with outdoor activities and skiing, so we phoned up a couple of the estate agents and one of them said that Ariège is absolutely beautiful.'

I'd been wondering how far the internet was encouraging people to purchase property in areas they weren't at all familiar with. Before the web, prospective buyers must surely have driven around, getting a feel for places, whereas now it seems like people feel satisfied with making their discoveries via the screen. 'We did a little bit of research on the computer, to see what the area's got to offer, and that was all really. We've had to rely on the internet since because we haven't been here on site to project manage the work.' Nevertheless, the internet had been slow to trickle down to this corner of France. 'Email hasn't really arrived here, and with our architect that was a big problem because he only did faxes. We had to go and buy a fax machine because he didn't understand the internet.'

This was 2011 and I'd been aware that there were still pockets of local resistance to the digital revolution; Juliette had told me she'd chased off a couple of men in suits who'd been knocking on doors to talk about bringing the internet to the valley. 'We don't want those sort of changes here,' she'd said, although her children sometimes knocked on my door to make use of my mobile broadband. And I'd heard of a demonstration in Massat where locals had lain down in the road to protest against new mobile network masts.

It was becoming common to find one spouse reliant on the other for speaking the local language. Some slight frustrations emerged from Lynn about the pressures of being the one who speaks French, and Steve's difficulty in grasping even the basics; he "just about does a *oui*". 'When letters come through the post, when the phone rings, it's thrown at me straight away, even when I'm in the shower.' She was still at the stage of having a fear of phones. 'I hate it. I look at the number and think, do I or don't I?' She took a sharp intake of breath. 'It depends on what mood I'm in, whether I answer it or not.'

I was beginning to notice that those whose French was developed beyond a basic level often displayed the least confidence, and vice versa. Pat and John came across as happy with their fairly basic French, blaming communication breakdowns on the recipient's lack of understanding. Yet Gerald, whose competence was the envy of the other incomers, spoke regretfully about not having that 100% understanding. And now Lynn was admitting to not answering the phone if she didn't feel up to it, despite being able to hold down a job as well as converse with the local French, who sounded as if they were lurking around to talk to her all the time. 'On the campsite it got to the stage where we were having to duck behind the caravan and walk along the top to avoid them all, because they don't just stop and say, *Hi, you alright?* An hour later you're still there, engaging in conversation.'

LIKE HEBDEN BRIDGE

The idea that English migration to France was a middle-class phenomenon was beginning to show its cracks here in the foothills of the Pyrenees. I don't doubt that the majority of British incomers in France would fit somewhere within the centre of our social class scale, but it was clear that things in the Ariège were a little different. Pat had positioned herself as scornful of the Muriels of Mirepoix, using an unmistakeably posh accent to voice them, and Tina had also placed herself apart from the wealthier Brits with their pre-dinner drinks overlooking the pool. Now, as the cement mixer whirred, Lynn began to describe how they were not like the other English who came to France. 'We're very ordinary, very working class background. There's no airs and graces about us, what you see is what you get.' I gathered that she'd felt some concern that the other English out here might be the opposite, "a little bit more public school type", which is why she'd become excited when an English estate agent had told her that the Ariège was "very much like Hebden Bridge, a very hippy area" in the north of England. 'You can see in the way people dress around here, and I thought, yeah, this'll probably suit us better. I'm not into pretentiousness.'

Like the others, Lynn used the Dordogne as a benchmark. 'I think people come here because they don't want that Dordogne thing. They want to take part in the French culture. They don't want the English on the doorstep all the time. It's ok to be friendly, but not to rely on them and fall heavily on them, which I think is what happens in the Dordogne.' She also associated the place with a kind of higher class "pretentiousness", having experienced some of this in a French class back in England. 'They were all so pretentious and it was so la-di-da,' she laughed, 'and I just thought *oh God.*' She then put on a posh accent, saying, 'They said *where's your land, where've you bought then?* And they said *Ohhh, where's that, I haven't been to the Ariège.* And nobody knew it! And I thought, *well, you won't because you probably haven't stepped outside your villa in the Dordogne.* They were in just a completely different league to me.'

It was hard not to laugh at the plummy vowels and imagine the rest of the class shaking their heads at this place in France they'd never heard of. More seriously, I began to see the deckchairs and the sprayed graffiti as a stab at class counter-culture. Lynn and Steve were making a statement and not just of who they were, but of who they *weren't.* They didn't have a villa among the other middle-class Brits, a neat house with a neutral public face. Their own house, standing rather grandly in the valley, had been brought down to earth with its graffiti and its English name.

I showed Lynn the teashop menu and she smiled at it. 'It's like they're trying to cater for both the English and the French there,' she laughed. 'We do like our carrot cake, don't we?' I sat waiting for the contempt that everyone else so far had brought in, and when it didn't arrive I pointed out that others had turned up their noses at the clumsy mix of English and French, saying that they would never go in there. 'Really?' she said, genuinely aghast. 'Why would that offend me? It's like I say, the sort of person I am, I wouldn't be offended by that.' Her next comment foreshadowed the regrets about missing English culture that she would raise with me the following summer. 'What I really miss is the takeaways. Ringing up on a Saturday night and thinking let's get a Chinese, let's get an Indian or I'll nip into the fish and chip shop. There's none of that. That would be heaven.'

It was all part of that contradiction that lay just beneath the surface of people's experiences: on the one hand they enthused over what they liked about France and its customs, claiming like Lynn to want to engage in French culture. At the same time they continued to hanker after what was familiar to them from the old life. And this was why *Life in France, in English* sometimes went no further than viewing it as a voyeur, from a convenient distance; engaging in French culture through the window.

Back to the following summer, when I was being shown around the almost-completed house that was already up for sale. For Lynn and her partner it was the end of a dream, one that they admitted they'd approached the wrong way. She gestured towards the plunge pool. 'After the stress of working all I want to do on my day off is sit in that, but Steve gets annoyed because I'm not helping with the house,' she said. She described the long drive to work on twisting roads in the dark winter months, to a job that was well below the level and the salary that she had been on back in England. Having to fight for the occasional day relaxing in an inflatable plunge pool while your partner tried to drag you inside to decorate was not the idyllic life she'd have imagined. It was also clear that living a long way from English friends and family had hit them hard. The first time I spoke with her, she'd been adamant that they wouldn't be looking to spend time with other English people, but the reality was that they missed them. The St George flag deckchairs, the "Welcome to Valley Cottage" graffiti and even the English house name were symbols of who and what they still were, but they also conveyed an attempt to broadcast their Englishness. Viewed from the roadside, the graffiti in particular was an invitation – perhaps even a plea – to passers-by. *We're English, please stop and talk to us!*

I could understand how that idea of France as a "return to Britain in the 1950s" might be compelling if you'd grown uncomfortable with modern-day Britain, but it was hardly an idyllic life if you had to earn a living doing whatever was available from a limited range of options. The laid-back anti-commercialisation of the Ariège was described by forum members as part of its allure, but here was Steve complaining about the shops closing at lunchtime. People were eager to reinvent themselves as adventurous, appreciative of another culture and what it symbolised, and in defining who they were, they drew heavily on the idea of avoiding the other Brits and British culture. But our capacity for adaptation can be limited by those enduring aspects of the self, our long-standing routines and attitudes, some of which we might not even want to change. As one male retired member said to me, 'You can't just forget all these things that you've grown up with and been used to.'

Some of this had been acknowledged by incomers on the online forum, those who recognised the contradictions between portraying a more independent, integrated and linguistically competent lifestyle, and taking comfort from the familiar English community. One member had summed it up by warning a "newbie" member who was about to arrive: *Do not be too dependent on British people. I realise that it is more comforting to mix with the rest of the expat residents, but try to get a balance between the two.* The newcomer replied that they were *not going to become dependent on anybody*, but she then justified her offline networking requests as logical, claiming it was *important to get the comfort from expats as these are the people who know how things work in England. They know what problems and differences we may be up against when we arrive.*

Trying to conceal your bacon-buying or your socialising with other English incomers were really quite minor issues that were mostly about what kind of person you wanted to be seen as. But the gap between appreciating French family culture and moving away from your own was one that I was finding it difficult to get my head around. Pat and John had justified it in terms of having "done their bit"; after years of working and bringing up children, now the focus was on time for themselves. For Tina, with a teenage daughter in the UK, she'd pointed out the difference between the perceived ease of getting a quick flight back and the actual reality of coping with airports, flight schedules and time off work. Bringing children over to the Ariège didn't always work out either; I'd heard over and over about one particular family with teenage girls who'd recently returned to the UK after two years of "roughing it" in the middle of nowhere. A key factor seemed to be the unhappiness of one daughter; a teenager who "hated it and made their life a living hell", according to the gossip. Even Lynn had come across the family during her first few months in the Ariège, describing them as "normal, down-to-earth people" whom she'd have enjoyed spending time with if only they'd stayed. She filled me in with the details as we sat next to the house foundations. 'They took on such a huge project, to build a house with a gîte. The parents loved it but the eldest girl struggled like mad to a point where she was desperately unhappy.' But that wasn't all. 'The two adults were living in a tent and the two girls were in a bit of a ramshackle place, to be honest, which was dirty and awful. And then the land they were building on had a landslide.' It sounded badly planned. Lynn nodded. 'They did it on a whim apparently. They came out, they loved it, they sold up and then bought the land after they'd moved here. They just decided *let's go*, and that was it.'

I got ready to leave. 'Come back one evening,' she said, 'I do a great spaghetti Bolognese.' I thanked her, privately hoping that I'd been placed into the category of "normal, down-to-earth people" rather than that of the pretentious la-di-das.

Lynn and Steve eventually returned to the UK, although, as is often the case in the Ariège, the house took a few years to sell. Some two years after Lynn told me that the house was going on the market I happened to have lunch with the estate agent handling the sale. Janneke, an English-speaking agent favoured by many of the Brits, told me that she was shifting plenty of lower-priced houses, but that beautiful detached house in the sunny valley had received hardly any viewers to date. It seemed a shame, as in some respects Lynn and Steve had achieved what others craved; a spacious house that wasn't a money pit, and employment with the French. But it wasn't enough to keep them there.

SWIMMING IN ARSENIC

On the way back I decided to cool off by doing what I'd seen others do and plunged into the transparent waters of the river

Salat, at a point downstream of the rapids where the river bed dropped low enough to be able to swim. The previous week I'd stopped the bike to sit on a low wall overlooking the river and watch a couple in the water, shifting my gaze slightly when I realised that they were swimming naked. Today I'd come prepared to test the water and had followed a track on the opposite bank that led to a flat rocky platform, perfect for lowering oneself into the water. Just one other bather was there today, a solitary woman who lay reading in a bathing suit. We nodded at each other as I positioned myself at a tactful distance. The peace was momentarily broken by a line of mules who stepped past, laden with the baggage of a party of children who were following noisily behind. The young woman leading the mules stopped right in front of me to cup her hands and drink from the clear water, and when they'd all moved on I lowered myself in, trying not to gasp too loudly at the temperature. The Salat flows down from the heights of Mont Rouch above Salau, and is later joined by others such as the Garbet, the Arac and the Lez before they all go on to feed the Garonne further north. As I swam, the numbing sensation of glacial cold was broken by the gentle push of the current as it massaged my arms and legs. It would have been easy to give in to it and be carried downstream towards Seix.

As with any other river fed by vast uplands, the Salat can change dramatically in a short time. Further upstream was the village of Salau, the site of a former tungsten mine that had closed in 1986. One July I'd walked past the old mine workings on my way up to a vast ice cave that nestled in a glacial corrie, or cirque, above Salau. The old mine buildings were still there, empty and graffitied, and I'd dashed into one of them to shelter when a particularly violent storm had appeared out of nowhere. The skies lashed down so much rain that I watched in some alarm as the Cougnets, a tributary that fed the Salat, changed to a frighteningly angry torrent of brown that threatened to spill over the banks. I later read that this was exactly what had happened back in 1982, causing half of Salau to be destroyed with the force of the water.

There's currently a push to reopen the tungsten mines, with an Australian company, Apollo Minerals, coming in as a partner to help fund the feasibility study. Besides the financial attractiveness of extracting the tungsten deposits, the mines were also known to contain copper and gold. I don't suppose I was the only one alarmed at the idea of commercial vehicles trundling their way up and down the narrow valley road, but the local community had focused on a more sinister factor: the known presence of asbestos in the mines. This was casting the darkest shadow of all over the scheme. Local inhabitants felt that they'd been left out of any consultations within a project where too much had gone on without official authorisation. And if the threat of asbestos wasn't enough, there was a perceived risk of pollution to the environment from the existing PCBs left behind in the original mine galleries, not to mention the use of cyanide to extract gold.

Thirty or so protestors at the demonstrations might sound as if locals weren't particularly bothered about the issue, but the commune itself had fewer than a hundred inhabitants, and something like 80% of its houses were secondary residences. The original mine employees had largely moved away after the mine closed, leaving just ten inhabitants in the village at that time. More recent incomers had chosen the valley for the particular lifestyle and "protected environment" that it offered, which all seemed rather vulnerable now. The usual mantra about development bringing employment opportunities was completely pointless here, as everyone knew that mining experts from elsewhere would be brought in to work the deposits. It had come as a shock to some of the incomers that they'd moved close to somewhere with a hidden cocktail of arsenic, asbestos, cadmium, zinc and hydrocarbons, and naturally they worried that reopening it would endanger the Salat watershed. Yet, as someone commented ironically, hikers have long been drinking from the river and its tributaries, totally unaware of what might be invisible within that clear glacial water. Yes, I thought, and they swim in it, too.

A PAST ENCOUNTER

The van was old, with a British registration plate, and some part of its suspension had collapsed, causing it to lean alarmingly towards the edge of the road that fell away down the slope. The road itself was so narrow that the lurching van blocked it, and a gathering of impatient people and their vehicles had built up to the front and rear. I recognised some locals, such as the forest ranger in his waders, on his way out for a fishing trip, but I had never before seen the tattooed lady in a black hat and heels, who was raging about being late for her *rendez-vous*. A young, scruffy Irishman rifling through the chaos inside the van turned out to be the owner, Dylan, urgently searching for his insurance details. It turned out that Dylan and his South American girlfriend Anna had purchased some land complete with tumbledown barns with the idea of setting up an eco-camp. They were in the process of building a couple of yurts to rent out to people who would appreciate the tranquillity of staying miles away from anywhere. Unfortunately they'd failed to take into account that the land had no road access to it, apart from a private road owned and built by a man known locally as *L'Ours* (The Bear). The Bear didn't see why he should let scruffy newcomers benefit from his hard labour, and so Dylan and Anna were left to carry everything, including two large wood-burning stoves, up a steep track, accompanied by their three-year-old toddler. It didn't seem to have occurred to them that paying visitors might find the whole access thing a bit awkward.

Dylan and Anna seemed as curious about us as we were about them, and after my partner Terry helped to nudge the van over so that the other cars could get past, they invited us up to see their place that night. Their land turned out to be almost vertically above my own house, and Dylan had begun improving the access by tying a muddy rope to a tree, which made it only slightly easier to haul oneself up onto a track that was littered with boulders from the collapsing terrace walls on either side. The track soon became a strenuous climb past a few derelict barns, and all I could think of was how on Earth Dylan had managed to haul log burners up here. After twenty minutes or so we finally came out into a small clearing and saw the randomly painted woodwork of their barn and the beginnings of a yurt that were emerging from a wooden platform close by.

Dylan showed us around his land, which was extensive but steep and forested. It included a second building much further up the hillside, another barn that was ostensibly a more habitable structure than the one they were living in, but unfortunately graced with a large bulge in one of the exterior corners where the mortar-less stones had moved outwards. 'I never noticed that when the estate agent showed us round,' admitted Dylan, 'but it should be easy enough to fix with acros.' That was true, but the manner of getting acros up to that spot was another matter. I felt a bit vulnerable with the weight of the entire house above my head and was relieved when Dylan led us out, locking the door with an ancient and enormous key.

We skidded back down the hillside to the barn where we sat on an old car seat in their "living room", breathing in the fumes from one of the wood-burning stoves close by. Dylan's attempt to install a dormer window was pointed out with good humour, as something they were learning to do as they went along. All the time the lights flickered on and off, as they were powered by car batteries and it was easy to accidentally nudge the wires. Up a ladder we went to see the bedroom, which was a tent *inside* the roof space, the tent offering essential protection from an existing family of *loirs,* or edible dormice, who had taken residence in the upper rafters. These original occupants harassed the human family all night long, screeching and throwing nuts at them as they tried to sleep. As Juliette said, it was understandable because the *loirs* had been there first and would resent the humans moving in to their territory. She also implied that the creatures would know the difference between a house, which was meant for human habitation, and a barn.

Running water was a permanently open tap fixed to the end of a hose that dangled in a stream, powered by nothing more than gravity. I was impressed by their attempts to make the camp homely, and Anna had been busy putting colourful paint onto the exterior woodwork, but everything seemed to be done in the wrong order; aesthetics before essentials. In the twilight the enormous trees that overshadowed the clearing made it seem a gloomy place, and it was plagued by mosquitoes. We left Dylan sitting staring into the flames of the second log burner that had been installed outside the house like a patio heater. 'I'll sit here and watch "television" for a bit,' he said, 'but come back tomorrow evening and we'll have something to eat.'

THANK YOU FOR THE FOOD

Another couple were visiting the following evening, although they'd chosen to sleep in their van, parked below, blaming the unbearable mosquitoes that were "eating them alive". It was Anna's childhood friend Maria, here with her partner, a silent man in a hat who mostly stared into a nettle salad without eating or drinking anything. Our offering of cooked pasta and a bottle of wine were viewed with what looked like suspicion. 'I only drink water,' said Anna, but she went to fetch us a couple of jam jars for the wine. Anna admitted that they hadn't yet sought permission to convert the barn into something that was officially habitable. 'We don't really know what we're doing,' she laughed. 'We're like children, you know?' I wondered how long before it would end in tears or worse; the attempt at constructing a dormer window was one thing but the amateurish installation of a wood stove was a bit worrying.

We stood up to go back down before it got too dark to negotiate the path and the rope. The silent man looked up and nodded goodbye with a "thank you for the food".

'You're welcome,' I smiled, fully aware that he hadn't touched any of it.

I'd wondered how Dylan and Anna had found this obscure piece of real estate, and it turned out to be quite simple. They'd bought it from my next-door neighbours, Claude and Sandrine, who'd advertised it with the local estate agents as a way to fund the renovations of their semi-derelict holiday home. Claude, from Toulouse, had inherited a percentage of the property, along with a number of other relatives, when the previous elderly occupant had died. Claude was so keen to revisit the childhood holidays he'd spent here that he bought out the other inheritors and then sold off the less accessible land and barns to Dylan and Anna. He then set about making his own house more habitable. This involved finding a home for the vast amount of artefacts that his grandfather had collected over his lifetime on this hillside; the house was littered with cow bells of all sizes, a seated contraption for shaping wooden staffs and an ancient radio that blew up with a bang and a puff of smoke when Claude switched it on for us. He then pulled one of the wormy old chairs in front of the vast inglenook fireplace and sat on it, arms folded, to show us how the old man had spent his later years. The house put me in mind of a cave; the bare rock floor was uneven but polished from a hundred and fifty years of humans and cattle walking back and forth, and the bare stone walls glistened with damp that seeped through from the hillside.

Claude spent the next few years banging and cursing his way through the renovations, much of which looked fine to my ignorant eye, but which alarmed Juliette and Vincent, who tut-tutted at the new floor beams and the way he'd repaired the old wooden stairs with concrete. Claude insisted on doing everything himself, but it was a huge undertaking. One weekend he got close to seriously injuring himself when he threw the unwanted stuff into a bonfire that exploded, blackening his face and arms all over.

I noticed that Sandrine began to come down less and less often. According to Juliette she was uneasy in the mountains, disliking the roads and fearful of wildlife such as the adder that often bedded down in my stopcock pit. It was no great surprise when the house was put up for sale halfway through the renovations. Juliette shook her head. 'Whoever buys it will need to rip it out and start over again. It's all been done wrong.'

DINNER FOR ELEVEN

The next time I saw Dylan was during that sweltering late summer when I arrived back in the Ariège to travel around talking to the English incomers. I'd been hearing about the

Occupy Wall Street demonstrations, which were all over the news, and it had got me thinking about Dylan and his desire to escape the stress and consumerism of London by living out here in the wilds. It was thus a coincidence to see his battered old van parked at the end of the track, but there was another vehicle parked in my usual spot, a smaller white van that had its driver door left wide open, with no sign of the driver. Dylan walked over, dwarfed by a lanky, sunburned man whose long red hair was en route to dreadlocks. Dylan introduced him apologetically as the van owner, hoping that I wouldn't mind him using my space, and explaining that parking the car with the door ajar was a deliberate strategy to deter thieves from breaking in. 'They can see there's nothing to steal, so they won't bother to break in,' explained the newcomer, a Dutch man who introduced himself then laughed. 'Don't worry,' he said, 'no one can pronounce my name.' I tried it but he winced and Dylan laughed.

'We don't know what to call him!' he said. 'How about we give you an English name, something similar like Gerald or Graham?'

But the Dutch man frowned, shaking his head. 'Those are not nice names.' I found out that Vincent openly referred to him as Carotte, which seemed mean, and over the next few days I began to think of him as Stig, inspired by his story of building a house in the Netherlands using "everyone else's rubbish". He must have meant that he'd built it from recycling old building materials, but I'd naively envisioned a house constructed from landfill, stinking and lumpy with walls of rotting cartons and containers. That vision, plus his long straggly hair, had put me in mind of the childhood classic *Stig of the Dump*, and so to me, he privately became Stig.

Stig and Dylan had met at a festival somewhere and, as became apparent, Dylan had a tendency to invite everyone to his place here in the Ariège. Stig had been spending time in the neighbouring Aude, and after meeting Dylan he'd become excited by the description of the secluded hillside in a valley that had a reputation for *live and let live*. He'd arrived on the lookout for something more permanent in the area and joked about building up his property portfolio. At first I genuinely thought he was looking to buy something cheap, like Dylan and Anna, and I'd offered to introduce him to the Dutch estate agent who lived nearby, but this received only a blank expression. Eventually I clocked on to the fact that these "properties" were largely uninhabitable barns that he used as squats. He was looking for something a bit more comfortable than his Aude "house", which lacked a full roof and running water.

More people turned up over the next few days, as Dylan and Anna became the Pied Pipers of Massat. Their followers were mostly young travellers they'd met at festivals as well as random people they met in car parks. I met a stream of Italians, Israelis and French, all welcomed as labour to help erect the yurt that was taking shape on a wooden platform. I walked up there one evening to find most of them crammed into a gloomy makeshift kitchen inside the barn, elbowing each other and squinting as they concocted a dinner from what they'd salvaged from a supermarket skip that day. Early every evening they would cram into Dylan's van and head for one of Saint-Girons' supermarkets to rifle in the skips behind the store; an activity they referred to as "skipping". One of them would keep a lookout while the others rummaged for what they fancied taking. Most evenings as I returned home from interviewing the English, I would pass the van going the other way on its evening ritual. Tonight they proudly showed off the smoked salmon from that day's trip, and the girls swirled like dervishes in brightly coloured silk dresses that had also, unbelievably, been retrieved from a skip. I half imagined myself tagging along one evening, bumping around in the back of the van and doubling over to lean into the skips and pick out whatever took my fancy. But I knew I wouldn't be taken seriously and I didn't want to come across as self-indulgent, a voyeur playing at it. For them it was a way of life.

Stig and I left them to their cave-like kitchen and sat on tree stumps to share the bottle of wine I'd carried up. He confessed that the constant fighting between Anna and Dylan was already wearing him down. I knew that the valley was reverberating their bickering as their yells bounced all the way down the hillside; Juliette had asked them to be more considerate – "Please remember you're not the only people living here". Stig's solution was to move out to an empty house that he'd seen even higher up the mountain. This tiny, cave-like house had a window fabricated from a car windscreen and a bath outside. Everyone referred to it as "Andy's house". Juliet explained that Andy was a legendary English man who'd lived there for a while, and had been much admired for his strength and solitude, but who was now back in England living a more mainstream life.

I was astounded when Stig and Dylan managed to track down Andy via the internet to ask permission to use the house, which was granted. Stig declared it the most comfortable dwelling he'd had for years, undoubtedly charmed by the recycled car windscreen. He went on and on about having "running water" for the first time in ten years although, like Dylan's, it was just a hose from a stream. He told me how he liked to fill the bath in the morning so that the sun would warm it sufficiently by late afternoon. He would then enjoy an open-air soak, accompanied by a joint. I reminded myself not to go wandering up there unannounced.

I invited them all down to dinner one night, feeling intrigued by the way that they'd chosen to live. There was a vast difference between their humble way of life and that of the comfortably equipped English incomers with whom I was spending so much time, sitting in their manicured gardens and drinking tea brewed in teapots. I'd noticed Anna and the others gawping at my house with its flushing toilet, shower and mains electricity, knowing very well that I was outside the boundary of their usual social network. This was articulated very visibly when I dropped a piece of baguette on the ground and went to discard it; one of the girls grabbed it back, saying 'No, it's ok, it's us.' *Us*, not *you*.

That night I stood stirring a lentil dhal for a couple of hours, watching the light sink lower and wondering where they all were. Had I been stood up? Eventually they began to arrive in dribs and drabs, with Dylan and Anna arguing loudly over whose fault it was that some of the others hadn't followed them down. Dylan did his best to holler up the mountain with a yell that echoed round the valley as we all clasped our ears. I had assumed they'd all turned their noses up at anything as consumerist as a mobile phone, but then I saw Dylan get one out and look at it, shaking his head. 'Can you call them?' I asked.

'I would,' he said, looking sheepish, 'but we haven't bothered exchanging numbers.'

Anna strode into the house, introducing it to the toddler as if it were a museum– "Look! This is a real house!" – and leaving the child to bounce around on the furniture as if it were a novelty, which it probably was. Even Anna found it difficult to sit still, preferring to wrestle on the sofa with Antonio, one of the Italian youths.

Stig declared that he didn't like my house at all. 'It's too modern, I prefer the one next door,' he said. But he liked the food and he was the only one to really eat what I'd prepared. Juliette and Vincent shared a small dessert dish of dhal while most of the others just picked at it. But Stig demolished the dhal and then sat eyeing up the pear flan that Vincent had brought. Every time I offered him another piece he took it, until Vincent told him to just finish it off.

Stig wandered around looking at my photos of walks in the mountains, showing interest in the shots I'd taken of Goutets, a renovated summer village or *courtal* on a natural platform up in the summer pastures, or *estives*. I explained that it was now a protected heritage site where you could wander freely around the old stone huts. Dylan perked up his ears and suggested that perhaps we could all go up there and stay the night. I looked doubtful at the thought of us all traipsing up there and annoying the shepherds who were in residence throughout the summer. 'We can go for the day, there's no need to stay the night,' I said. 'If anyone wants to walk up for the day tomorrow, we can meet here.' A few of them nodded.

'We'll be here after coffee time,' said Stig. Eventually they all trudged back up the hillside, Dylan carrying the toddler, Anna and Antonio giggling together, and Stig carrying a torch and chimney brushes that he borrowed from me and promised to bring back the next day.

"After coffee time" was a vague nod to the morning gathering for coffee that took place at the unfinished yurt. In the end I waited until Stig and Antonio turned up just before lunchtime to walk up to Goutets. Stig expressed some anxiety that he was suitably dressed for a mountain excursion, perhaps expecting deep snow or a glacier. I reassured him that no special gear was required for a late summer excursion to the grassy summer pastures, and we set off.

It's possible to walk all the way up to Goutets via a stony access track that zigzags up the valley head, but that way is long and tedious with little of interest apart from a few ruined barns and a battered British Bedford van that's been abandoned by the roadside. Instead I led the other two across the hillside along forest paths that were steep but dappled with sunlight, and crunchy with acorn shells and the leaves of oak and beech. Stig stopped every now and then for a cigarette while Antonio told us of his dilemma; his parents wanted him to study a traditional subject at university, but he was fixated on the possibility of studying mind-bending drugs and their effects. I suggested that he think about the long-term opportunities offered by each of these fields of study, and then make a decision. He ran his way up to Goutets like a child, at one point vaulting over an electric fence to pull an apple off a tree, then spitting out the bitter fruit where he stood. When we finally reached Goutets they both turned their nose up at my stale bread and butter, preferring to stick to their smoked salmon sandwiches.

Goutets was built on a glacial platform just above the tree line and it's by far the most captivating of the *courtals*, as it's an entire network of small separate hamlets. Looking down from the platform you can trace the long route through the woods that you've just walked, whilst behind you're encircled by the immense ridge of the Pic de Trois Seigneurs. These summer villages were a feature of the Ariège landscape that grew and declined with the rhythm of the population. The combination of poverty and a population surge around the turn of the 18th–19th century encouraged people to move up to the higher Pyrenean valleys during the summer, taking their families and animals to live with them. Local people reminisced about huts built by their grandparents, and the days gone by when the extended family would go up for the summer, taking cows, sheep, pigs, goats and rabbits. The long summer days were spent tending the animals, making butter and cheese, and growing vegetables and hay for winter. Yet the same over-population led to many other inhabitants moving away from the area, starting a depopulation trend that was exacerbated by the First World War. In 1874, when my own house had been built, the population of my commune had been a little under 2,500, but by 1931 it had fallen to just over a thousand. Continuing to decline during the war and subsequent decades, it has languished below 200 since the mid 1970s.

After Goutets was abandoned in the 1960s, the efforts of the local *maire*, who happened to be a geography teacher, brought Goutets partially back to life. Jean-Louis Loubet garnered local manpower to partially restore some of the buildings, and it's now a protected heritage site, open to anyone with the time and energy to walk up there. One or two shepherds can be seen living up there in the summer months, watching the cattle and tending a small vegetable plot. Visitors who make the effort to hike up are charmed by the assortment of buildings, ranging from square dry-stone *cabanes*, or barns, with traditional slate-covered apex roofs, as well as more unusual smaller huts whose square walls are topped by a grassy-domed corbelled vault roof. This type of hobbit-style hut, known as an *orri*, was built with just eating and sleeping in mind, having little space beyond that needed for a bed frame. The rudimentary chimney was just a hole in the wall. Other huts were built to house chickens and pigs, while those that were built over a stream served as a basic fridge known as a *mazuc*, where the cold water kept the milk and butter chilled. Almost all of the huts have doors that remain unlocked and I showed Stig the old iron bed frame in one of them that still had its traditional mattress of dried ferns. He lay down on it, claiming it to be as comfortable as anything he had in his "houses".

The following week saw most of the visitors leaving the yurt camp until just Dylan, Anna, the toddler and Stig remained. Dylan was frantically trying to finish off the yurt, although the logic of completing it in order to leave it exposed to the snow on a wooden platform, at a height of 925 metres, escaped me. He admitted that he'd been dreaming of spending a winter here in isolation, looking down on a white world, although he must have known that the heavy snowfall and temperatures falling to minus 12 or lower would soon kill off any romanticism. Apart from that, the yurt had used up most of their money and he needed to go back to London to pick up more work.

Stig was also being drawn in to the vision of a solitary Pyrenean winter and had even talked about fetching a carload of books back from the Netherlands to see him though the long months up in Andy's house. But in the end common sense prevailed – for a start, the "running water" that had so charmed him would spend the entire season frozen solid.

In the end we all left the valley on the same morning, making our way in different directions; me to the airport at Toulouse, Dylan in his van rumbling the length of France towards the Channel and Stig to the more temperate Aude. The yurt had finally been finished and it sat proudly on its platform, superficially solid yet horribly vulnerable to the approaching winter.

Dylan, Anna and the toddler climbed into their van, while Stig and I shared a last coffee with Juliette and talked about what he called "our little community". It wasn't necessary to mention what an unconventional mix we were, but that very contrast, together with the unexpectedness of our time spent together, and our acceptance of each others' ways, was what now made it seem precious. We said our goodbyes, insisting we'd keep in touch but knowing deep down just how unlikely it was that our worlds would merge. Stig stooped down to return my hug, his musty ginger locks swinging around my face. 'Drive carefully,' I said, and he nodded.

'Always sixty, nothing more,' he replied. I followed his battered van down to Massat where we parted ways, blowing horns and waving animatedly while locals stood on the pavements and stared at us.

Dylan and Anna had come to this part of France seeking a life that was more fulfilling than what they had back in England. While Stig was a temporary visitor, he too had been drawn to the idea of settling there, at one point wondering whether he could make a living by growing and selling vegetables at the markets. There were certainly some faint parallels with the English incomers, as the essence of every move was a search for a more rewarding or meaningful life, whether they were looking for more simplicity or a challenge.

Sharing a bottle of wine outside with Dylan one night, while Anna had retired to bed with her jam jar of water, he talked about coming here to "find peace", hinting at an escape from something that remained unspoken. It was certainly a temporary relief from a grinding existence in London, but in the end, I suspected that they didn't have sufficient funds to do things properly. The land itself had been cheap for a reason; it lacked proper access and the habitation permit that would allow people to live there legitimately. Local officials turn a blind eye if people are living quietly and causing no disruption, but constructing yurts for paying visitors was a different thing altogether. Just as I'd seen with some of the English I'd met, things hadn't quite been thought through. The fact that something was initially affordable – in Dylan's case, a whole swath of land and two barns – meant that it probably had a lot of other issues that it was just too easy to overlook during the excitement of that first step. *We'll make it work.*

In the spring I ventured up to inspect the yurt and was saddened but not surprised to see that the weight of the snow had caused its destruction. Open to the elements, it was leaning at an angle, with the window frames shattered and the glass broken. Without getting too close I could see a miserable patchwork of sodden clothes, dripping hangings and books that were curled with damp. Jets of water spurted along the entire length of the hose that had provided their "running water" as it had been left in situ, undrained. I emailed Dylan to let him know, but he was already aware of the disaster. He'd offered the house to some friends, who'd done their best to clean up the sodden mess before leaving.

3

THE FRENCH RESISTANCE (AND RESISTING THE FRENCH)

———

I skidded on fallen chestnuts as I ran down the path from Dylan's camp, trying not to jolt my back as I stumbled over tree roots. I'd had a bounce on the trampoline next to the yurt, a toy that was used more by Anna than the toddler, but my ambitious attempt at a forward fall had jarred the length of my spine. I'd slunk off in agony, thankful that my graceless folly had gone unnoticed.

It was my final visit to Dylan's camp and Juliette and I had walked up together. We sat with Stig and Anna, huddled around a huge blackened kettle on an open fire, while Dylan shuffled around in his too-big orange waterproof, bringing us jam jars for the coffee and a length of *saucisse*. Autumn was beginning to break through, with less hazy but noticeably shorter days that began with a slight chill. As lunchtime approached I reluctantly took my leave, as I had an appointment to meet with a couple in one of the Saint-Girons cafés. 'Don't forget to ask them if they use English paint,' laughed Dylan. As someone who took whatever was available, he'd found the English insistence on their national brand of paint rather ludicrous.

I picked my way down the track, pondering the vast social divide between the people of this morning and those with whom I'd arranged to drink tea that coming afternoon.

Jim, Iris and I sat in the glass conservatory of the busy town centre café. I was aware that an odour of smoky bonfire still clung to me. 'I can't get on with some of the food here,' said Jim, shaking his head as he looked at the menu. 'I mean, for a country that makes so many cheeses I don't know why they can't make some really good ones.'

Iris looked over at me apologetically. 'He's so rude about the French people. So rude.'

Jim laughed, 'Ok, so that's a bit of a generalisation, but most of the cheeses seem to have been concocted out of a plastics factory. I just don't like that. I buy Cheddar from the Intermarché in Foix because you can buy Cheddar there. There are a few things like that that I really do miss, and the British shop here has pasted over some of the cracks, for getting just one or two of the bits you really miss.' The British shop was actually the reason we were sitting in the café; Iris had come in while I was chatting with Tina, and she'd offered to be interviewed, along with Jim.

Few of the people I spoke to admitted using the two British shops in the Ariège, yet Iris described their opening as a turning point that ended their isolation. 'We used to go to an English vet at Tarascon and he told us about a British shop starting up, and so we were one of her first customers. It's surprising how much better I felt because I did feel like I wasn't on my own anymore.' Her tone was of relief as she described being grateful for "the support".

The idea that one must avoid everything British, from people to food and shops, had been pervasive up to that point, so it came as a surprise when Iris spoke effusively about the British shops. In fact she showed bemusement when I asked if there was a stigma associated with them. 'Not a stigma, no, why?' she asked, adding that there wasn't always a local alternative to replace the things they missed. Iris particularly craved salad cream. They were helped out by friends who spent a few months in France at a time, bringing foodstuffs such as teabags as they drove "backwards and forwards". It was the first time that anyone had been happy to admit it, with Jim framing it as making the most of what's available.

'I don't see that it's a problem at all, really. I don't think you can draw a line under fifty years of being in a country and just change overnight.' Compared with Gerald he seemed unimpressed with the Ariège cuisine. 'I was disappointed for a long time... I didn't want to go out for meals, because past *cassoulet* you were struggling, but you do adapt a lot over time. But you can't just forget all these things you've grown up with and been used to.' Ariège seemed a bit of an odd choice for a couple who'd been used to dining out regularly.

I was even more struck when I heard that they'd chosen to move here without ever having visited the country. Like Pat and John, who'd drawn on the idea of challenge and adventure in early retirement, Iris had seen moving abroad as a way to avoid a waiting room for the retired. 'We lived on an estate in England for 27 years and I noticed towards the end of living there that I could see people sort of digging in to die. I can't put it in another way – they were having the soffits done with plastic so they didn't have to do those again. And I'm not ready to dig in to die.' I knew exactly what she meant. A colleague who was only a few years older than me had described how they'd replaced all of their furniture and had bought the best they could afford, as "it's probably the last furniture we'll need to buy". I understood the practicalities, but it made me shudder nevertheless.

The couple also admitted to a degree of reliance on the other Brits, with Jim describing the British network as "a sort of sounding board". Yet like everyone I spoke to, he showed awareness of the stereotype. 'We didn't want to go to somewhere that was going to be a British enclave. We did want to be somewhere that was going to be French.' It was the familiar story; wanting to avoid the Brits and live with the French, without having much idea at all about life in France.

Iris nodded in agreement. 'We wanted to avoid a British enclave,' she added before admitting, 'but we've ended up doing that, haven't we?'

Jim was swift to extricate them. 'Well, not really, no, not really, we're not involved with them every day. It's not like it's a continual sort of involvement with the Brits. As Iris said, for about six years we were totally, absolutely on our own.'

It was becoming clear that they'd reacted differently to their new home. Iris described herself as feeling extremely comfortable here in the Ariège, although the fact that Jim hadn't felt the same way had made it more difficult for her. 'It's tarnished my enjoyment for many years, because he hasn't felt the same. But in a nutshell I'd describe the Ariège as charming.' What was charming in her eyes came across as annoyingly old-fashioned in Jim's. He conveyed a sense of irritation, from the substandard cheeses to the frustration of getting things done in a place that he saw as 60 years behind the times.

'I still can't get used to the shops closing from 12 till 2,' he said, echoing Steve. He put it down to 25 years of working in a large multinational company that had instilled "a sort of discipline" that he couldn't let go in retirement. Conscious that he was coming across as dissatisfied, he checked himself and admitted that he often reminded himself not to take it for granted. 'The whole sort of lifestyle that we have now, the way that we enjoy where we are, the house, the privacy we have, the space and that sort of thing, you could never have back in the UK.' The couple didn't go back to England very often but when they did it brought things more clearly into relief. 'You get off the plane at Stansted, and you go and park on the M11, and you think, *Oh, this is why we left*. It brings it back to you. You do realise then and you appreciate the benefits.'

I couldn't get over the fact that they hadn't even visited France, let alone the Ariège département, before moving here. This sparked off some disagreement on why they'd ended up in this particular spot. Iris was keen to frame it as a more aesthetic search based on wanting to be near mountains, with a vague initial plan of letting out gîtes. 'It was just chance. We stuck a compass pin in a map and drew 40km radius circles around Toulouse and Carcassonne for the airports. I saw this house on the internet and loved it and that's how we ended up in the Ariège.'

Jim disagreed. 'There were some more practical reasons as well.'

'Not particularly for the Ariège, there weren't. It was by chance.'

'But it was also financial,' insisted Jim. 'We did some brief investigations here, and at that time it was really good value for money. So financially it was a good deal. We really wanted to make more of whatever investments we'd got. Our property in the UK bought us a lot more here, not just our house. We decided that letting gîtes was too much like hard work, and over the years we bought apartments that we run as long-term rentals but for the French people. So it was really trying to maximise whatever investment we'd got.'

Iris seemed unwilling to let them come across as hard-headed, commercially minded folk in search of the best deal. 'I think the Ariège in particular wasn't about investment. It was by chance, just where the house was.'

'Well, it was and it wasn't,' replied Jim, perhaps keen to avoid being seen as romantic and impractical. He tried bringing in other practical reasons. 'The mountains are one thing, but we still have the plan to do some more travelling. One of the reasons for looking here was that it was nice and central for getting around Europe.'

'Am I gonna get interviewed as well?' Len, a friend of the couple, interrupted the flow as he leaned over the table and proceeded to fill us in on the details of his recent cruise holiday to Greece. I heard all about where his money had gone; seven euros for a gin and tonic, fifty for a short excursion and eight euros per day compulsory tipping. He'd been especially put off by the communal eating arrangements on the cruise, aghast that people were queuing up to put spaghetti Bolognese and chicken wings onto their plates. 'When I saw the people eating I couldn't face it.' I sat there smiling politely, not wanting to appear rude but wondering if all of this detail could wait. Eventually he moved on. 'Gimme a shout,' he cried as he walked away.

Trying to paper over the disruption, I asked about the language. Iris had moved out with the O level French that she'd learned forty years ago, and had set about building on that. The couple had attempted to join the infamous French classes in Saint-Girons, where they admitted they "didn't learn a lot", but more importantly it had helped to broaden their circle of English-speaking friends. They'd spent most of their time in the classroom comparing notes with the other English incomers on various French processes.

Being the main French speaker meant that Iris was responsible for all the paperwork for their lettings business. Jim, however, drew on that vague notion of *getting by*; a phrase that the Brits used to refer to a wide spectrum of ability. 'I can get by, I can go and do most things now,' he said. 'But what I can't do is have a French conversation. Where I run into problems is where I go to speak to somebody and use a few words of French and of course it comes back like a machine gun.'

Their estate agent had told them an anecdote about a couple who'd come over without knowing any French at all. 'They were full of it, you know, they were full of it, and she was a very gregarious person but she couldn't speak French. Within less than a year she was in hospital, her nerves were shot. She developed mental problems because she couldn't socialise.'

'We don't socialise a massive amount,' said Jim. Nevertheless they spoke of the British circle with warmth and relief at having discovered a valuable support network. In contrast there was little reference to mixing with the French, and Jim admitted that they weren't really immersed in the French way of life. He saw this as due to a number of practical factors, such as not working or having children, which made it easy to avoid everyday mingling in the community. I asked whether they felt they shared anything culturally with the French, thinking back to the jolly get-togethers that Pat had said were essential for the Brits to avoid being seen as isolationist. Iris shook her head. 'We don't share in the French-type cultural things, do we? We've been very bad, we've not really done much.' Some of the responsibility was laid at the door of the locals, whose "closed" nature was explained as a legacy of wartime events. 'This area was a centre of resistance. One year 13 people were shot by the Germans and a nearby village was practically razed to the ground by the Germans because of the resistance activities.'

Once again Jim waded in with another practical factor that drew attention away from Iris' claim that they had not made any effort. He drew outlines with his finger on the table. 'No, I don't think that's the only reason. You've got the village here, and we're up over there, so we're not actually in the village.'

'Yes,' agreed Iris, 'but if we'd gone to the fête and that sort of thing we would have got to know people. We've not made that effort.' Like everyone else they'd repeated the formulaic factor of wanting to avoid British enclaves and to move to "somewhere French", but they seemed happy to observe it all from a distance. As long as they could buy the space, privacy and mountain view they wanted, and make some investment for a retirement income, the choice of France itself was of less significance. At least they were honest and didn't pretend that they'd slotted into the French community, happily citing their own lack of effort, as well as the *froideur* of the local French.

I finished my coffee and took out the photograph of the Mirepoix café menu, wondering what kind of reaction I'd get from people who regularly shopped for British-branded goods. Iris frowned. 'No, there's too much written in English. It would put me off.'

'It's in Mirepoix,' I said.

Iris nodded, recognising it now. 'We tried to go there. I'd heard it was nice to go to and we went one day, but it was closed, wasn't it?' She turned to Jim. It was a familiar reaction; people turning their noses up at the menu and claiming that they would boycott it. But everyone seemed to have gone out of their way to visit it.

'Let us know when you're this way again and we'll go for a pizza,' said Iris as we parted. 'We'll show you a really good pizzeria in town.'

A LIFESTYLE CHANGE THAT
YOU KNOW NOTHING ABOUT

On the drive back I pondered what seemed, to me, to be a bizarre decision to choose an unfamiliar country for a new life. Once again I was put in mind of the power of the media – especially television programmes such as *A Place in the Sun* – in propelling people towards a new life in France. *Why shouldn't we do that? Let's be adventurous! There's more to life than...* But the TV shows almost invariably ignore the practicalities of real life, being focused on showing properties that "tick all the boxes" in places where "your money goes further". I couldn't remember *ever* seeing any sign of neighbours or people in the background. Presumably the setting is cleansed of locals for the filming, giving the impression of a nice empty environment for the English to slot into. The issue of it being a country where another language is spoken is almost always skirted over. Prospective buyers always stated that they wanted to integrate with the locals and learn the language, but it wasn't that simple.

I managed to track down the instalment of *A Place in the Sun* that Lynn had mentioned, the one featuring Massat that had been filmed in 2008 and was titled *Ceredigion versus Couserans*. The couple were Steve and Lisa, who were planning "an absolutely huge lifestyle change", with plans to live off the land and become self-sufficient. The programme was focusing on whether this huge change would take place in Wales or Ariège. Steve had some familiarity with the Couserans region, but, true to the genre, there was absolutely no mention of the French language, or of any practical aspects of the area beyond the views from the property windows. If anything, the practicalities focused on Wales, which seemed illogical when self-sufficiency would surely have been a much more challenging project for a British couple landing in the depopulated, French-speaking Couserans. For all I know Steve and Lisa could have been French speakers with a good idea of what kind of life they'd be living as subsistence farmers in the Massat valley. Yet the presenter gave it away when she referred to buyers like them "taking on a lifestyle change that you know nothing about". The couple admitted that they were looking forward to "a big adventure, with lots of mistakes along the way".

I have to remind myself that these programmes are made for entertainment rather than any kind of advice, but nevertheless they *are* taken seriously by viewers who just see a property search in a stunningly beautiful area and a bit of negotiation to knock a few thousand off the vending price. The superficiality was intensified when the "beautiful mountain village of Massat" was accompanied by images of a completely different place: the stations of the cross stretching up the hillside from the church of Notre Dame de Raynaude, some 33km distant.

RESISTANCE

Mulling over my conversation with Iris and Jim, I'd wondered about the supposed link between the wartime resistance activities in the area and the "closed" nature of the locals, wondering if it was an easy excuse for their lack of socialisation. However, it turned out that they were not the only people to believe this. Another English incomer, living in the same area, independently commented to me about the continuing suspicion and even animosity between former collaborator and resistance families in the same area, and has also written about it.[16]

---

16   http://www.grillou.com/articles/once-upon-a-time-rimont-ariege-1944

In fact, the episode that Iris referred to has become one of the more notoriously cruel events that took place as the war drew to a close, one that left the village of Rimont with horrific memories and the designation of *village martyr*. That part of the Ariège had an active *résistance maquis* based around the Col de la Crouzette, who were regularly in conflict with local supporters of the occupation, particularly the Milice – a small but ruthless French militia drawn from supporters of the far right. Edward Stourton has described in detail how the event demonstrates a kind of blindness, or unwillingness to face up to the inevitable, among the collaborators. The event appears to have been sparked off by the assassination of a prominent local resident, Paul Laffont, by fascists on the 13th July 1944. The following retaliation on a list of collaborators drawn up by the maquis included acting on false information that had been given maliciously, as well as the simple mistake of shooting the wrong person at the wrong address. Such "errors" have no doubt sustained a foundation of resentment between some of the families.

Yet worse was to follow for the village of Rimont. As the Allied landings set the liberation of France in motion, German troops began to evacuate the Ariège mid-August. Some towns were liberated following their departure, whilst others suffered from those who continued to fight. Saint-Girons, for example, had its liberation complicated by the arrival of around two thousand reinforcements that included Soviet prisoners from the Legion of Turkestan. They moved on to Rimont on the 21st August, augmented by sympathisers and collaborators, where they forced their passage by shooting villagers, raping women and systematically setting fire to all buildings in the village and surrounding areas.[17] The Germans surrendered the following day, but it was too late for Rimont – eleven civilians and four

---

17   www.resistance-ariege.fr

maquisards had been killed, while some 236 buildings had been destroyed.

There was the usual rounding up of collaborators after the liberation of the Ariège towns, with suspected denouncers shot in towns like Saint-Girons. In the frenzy of *l'épuration* – the purge – the divisions and the tragic mistakes fuelled local resentment that would have taken a long time to fade away. So perhaps the events of so long ago really were continuing to affect the way in which the community interacted in and around the *village martyr* – with suspicion being the normal way of life, and quite possibly affecting how newcomers were accepted.

However, I'd also been reminded that the continuing influence of the past in how newcomers were accepted was not confined to wartime events. There could also be a lack of shared understanding between what the long-standing villagers saw as the normal, indeed the only, way to live, and the trend to live a more mobile lifestyle, uprooting to a country one had no connection with. The same incomer who'd confirmed the continuing divisions in Rimont described this dislocation as a significant factor that could affect relations between the locals and the incomers. If the concept of upping and moving country, or even region, was an alien concept to the villagers, then it could understandably form a barrier between incomers and those whose families have lived in the same locality for generations.

And yet... Ariège has seen more emigration than most départements in France, so the concept of moving away to live would surely not be totally unfamiliar to the Ariégeois. What *might* be unfamiliar would be the reasons behind the move. In broader terms, people moved both in and out of the Ariège for "a better life", with locals fleeing the poverty and lack of employment. Yet for incomers like Iris and Jim, with money to invest, the Ariège was seen as offering a particularly good business opportunity for buying up cheap property to rent out.

IN THE STEPS OF PISTON AND HIS "TROUT"

While looking into the events described by Iris, I'd had little inkling that my own village had a wartime history linked to a well-known member of the resistance, and, moreover, that I had unknowingly been walking a route he'd used to smuggle escapees over the Pyrenees to Spain. The Ariège Pyrenees had a number of routes that had been operational for wartime escapees to Spain as well as earlier evaders fleeing Spain in the 1930s. The most well-known of these routes had opened as an official hiking trail in 1994. *Le chemin de la liberté* had an annual four-day commemorative hike, that until recently had been organised by the late Scott Goodall, a British man who'd settled in the area.[18] The Freedom Route had been featured on a BBC radio programme and described in Edward Stourton's painstakingly researched book on the wartime activities in the Ariège. More recently, the route had been featured within Channel 4's series *WWII's Great Escapes: The Freedom Trails*.

There was even a dedicated museum to the route, which I visited at the former site of the railway station in Saint-Girons. With just a receptionist watching television, I had the place to myself and wandered around the boards, discovering that some 33,000 French and 6,000 Allied service personnel had escaped over the Pyrenees, with 782 of the former said to have used Ariège routes. From 1943 anyone attempting to flee to Spain would have had to pass under cover of night through a Reservation Zone created by the Germans. This zone, some 20km deep, ran parallel with the frontier just north of the

---

18   *The Freedom Trail* (2005) by Scott Goodall.

Pyrenean chain, strung out along the German posts within the settlements of Sentein, Seix, Oust, Aulus les Bains, Auzat, Tarascon and Vicdessos. Freedom of movement was limited to those granted a circulation permit. Many of the isolated barns that were still dotted around had sheltered would-be escapees, sometimes for weeks or months on end.

All of this helped a continuing commemoration of the guides and helpers who'd risked their lives. It also contributed to the sense of Ariège being wild and untamed, resistant to the decrees of the central powers, and as a form of tourism it was seen as something to encourage. In the spring of 2017 there had been a call by the National Office of War Veterans and Victims in Ariège to develop more of what they termed commemorative tourism, asking for suggestions of lesser-known places and routes that might have potential. The Freedom Trail and its related museum were held up as exemplars of the kind of activity relevant to young and old, visitor and local, bringing more visitors to the Ariège but also satisfying the need to remember victims of conflict and war veterans.[19] At the same time I couldn't help wondering whether these reminders were helping to maintain the open wounds within the towns and villages where not everyone had been on the same side. I noted that in Rimont there had been an association set up in 1996 to create a museum relating to the Resistance and the Liberation, again to attract visitors but also to make a more substantial commemoration. The museum had yet to see the light of day.

It's true that there were other Ariège routes used by evaders to flee to Spain, and they had been overlooked in the attention given to that other famous trail. Gradually, and unwittingly at first, I began to build up clues that built up a picture of events much closer to my own doorstep. It all began when I zigzagged up a section of the long distance GR10 path to the summit

---

19 *La Depeche,* 28 March 2017.

of Mont Ceint, at 2088m. Expecting the usual iron cross on the summit, I was surprised to see instead a contraption that looked more like a parking meter. It was actually a notice, crudely painted in red with a protective hood and a glass jar containing a visitors' notebook, all of this held together by a lot of wire. The spidery red handwriting marked the 2014 ascent by an 85-year-old – Jean-Marie Claustre – but it also went back in time to tell how, in 1943, as a 14-year-old shepherd he would climb the peak to survey the land for German patrols. Any information would be passed on to help the *passeur* (smuggler) using the escape route via Pic des Trois Comtes. Claustre had actually placed the crude plastic sign on the summit back in the mid 1990s, regularly ascending the mountain to replace the visitor notebooks as they filled. Back then I had no idea that I'd already spent time walking along the same escape route that Claustre had been helping to protect.

The *passeur* in question turned out to be one of the most well-known of the Ariège smugglers: Jean Bénazet, a Varilhes mechanic who went by the codename *Piston*. Bénazet successfully smuggled 61 evaders in the earlier part of 1943, recording them as "trout" in his logbook, until his group was apprehended by a German ambush within the Garbet valley on the 13th June. Bénazet himself managed to escape and continued to assist local efforts, before he made his way to Toulouse and joined the Resistance. After the war he took up his job as a mechanic but also became a councillor, and died in 1991 at the age of 87.

The escape route used by Bénazet had passed through my own commune, which itself had been a centre of resistance. The maquis group, known as Le Port-Ezes, had used the village of Ezes on the opposite side of the valley as a base. A tiny hamlet strung out high up the valley, Ezes nowadays is a place where the children "live wild", according to Juliette, perhaps mindful of a catastrophe back in 2001 when one of two four-year-olds playing in a barn had died when it caught fire. I'd wandered up there one sunny winter's day, feeling chilled by the loss of the sun's rays as the encircling ridge had blocked them out by lunchtime. It was a place tinged with tragedy. Back in September 1943 the maquis group had come to a bloody end after being infiltrated by a "comrade" who turned out to be a member of the Milice. The subsequent arrival of 80 Germans to the hamlet led to arrests, deportations and the murder of the mother of one of the maquisards. This apparently was what led Piston to believe that he was under suspicion, prompting his relocation to Toulouse.

With the call for more commemoration activities to be organised, I wondered why more had not been made of this route, particularly with its connection to one of the more celebrated passeurs. After talking to locals and reading the odd online account, I began to piece parts of the route together. According to Fred Sabourin,[20] Piston would pass though Massat and then take a mule track, looking out for certain washing lines; if clothes were hanging, then it was safe to pass. The route then went up to the lake at étang de Lers and then crossed down to Coumebière, where evaders would ascend the Garbet valley, after which the climb became steep and dangerous up to the frontier.

Setting out from Massat, I followed a narrow track beside the River Arac before coming out onto the road that ran parallel. I stayed close to the verge to avoid the hundreds of bikes racing down the hill through the rain puddles towards me. It was La Casartelli and the road had been closed to vehicles for the duration of the race; convenient for the cyclists, but tiresome for the hitchhiker walking ahead of me, whose bare brown legs paced out from beneath the waterproof cape

---

20   http://www.fredsabourin.com/article-passeur-de-liberte-59665554.html

that was stretched over the hump of a rucksack, a cape that was dripping despite the shelter of his umbrella. As I drew up alongside he turned to greet me, offering me a share of the umbrella. He was making his way to visit a friend, starting with a low-cost bus from the north of France – "dix euros de Lille à Toulouse!" – followed by the kindness of drivers once the public transport options ran out. Now, with the road closed, he could only complete the last few miles on foot, in the rain. I offered sympathy but he shook it off, reminding me that the land was finally getting the rain that it needed.

Once we'd parted ways I carried on, losing sight of the cluster of houses up at Ezes and looking out for a track leading away from the road up to Courtignou. Nothing was marked but I took my chances and scrambled down a bank to follow a path along the stream, through the beech woods until the ground opened out into a clearing on the slope. By this time the rain had stopped and the sun began to shine through a gap in the low cloud, my route up the valley now a golden beam.

The next section that I walked began at the plateau de Coumebière, a starting point for many walks, including sections of the GR10. "Plateau" had initially seemed an incongruous name for a spot halfway up the winding pass road and encircled by ridges. It was only when I looked down onto Coumebière from above that I saw it as a wide, treeless ledge that plunged towards the valley of the Garbet, the void met by ridge after mountainous ridge that ran parallel to the horizon.

One could spend a week just walking the paths that radiate out from Coumebière, with the most visible being the zigzag of the GR10 carved like a single shoelace into the hillside. Once at the Port de Saleix there's an option to walk up to the panoramic summit of Mont Ceint, or continue south along the GR10. A third option is a rollercoaster of a long, long ridge that rises and falls as it switches through changing terrain, starting with a steep rocky climb and the narrow arête of the Cabanatous ridge, where I once temporarily lost my nerve and sat overlooking the drop to try and talk myself back. The next minute you're running along a grassy ridge overlooking the string of blue lakes at Bassiès to the left, before the path switches back to a scramble over faintly pink boulders, with a final stiff limb to the half-dome summit of Pic Rouge de Bassiès.

Today, however, I was following a lower route in the direction taken all those years ago by Piston and his "trout", along a narrow path that led to the tiny étang de Labant. There I overtook a woman stepping over rocks wearing the kind of neoprene fabric shoes worn by surfers. I guessed she was planning to swim and hadn't thought about needing something more appropriate and less painful for the 40-minute hike to get there. Ascending the ridge behind the lake, the landscape opened out to a heart-stopping panorama high above the Garbet valley, with the town of Aulus les Bains huddled down on the right, and on the left a mesmerising view deep into the glaciated valley head of the Garbet. The path to the étang du Garbet – the lake that feeds the river – is a little-marked track that runs parallel, and at times a thousand feet above, the valley floor, crossing the truncated spurs cut by glaciers. The lake gets its share of visitors, including families out for a day's fishing or a swim in the icy water. Yet I've never seen anyone else on that upper path. Most walkers prefer to start lower down and tackle a longer but less exposed climb up through the woods.

The first time I walked it was in November, when the first snowfall lay melting on the ground and the encircling walls of glaciated rock were ribboned with white. The path was narrow and I had to keep reminding myself not to plant my hiking pole as there was nowhere for it to go; a slip on the path would almost certainly result in a long tumble down to the Garbet. The snow made it difficult to even be sure that there was a path ahead, with only a faint stretch to be made out skirting along a kind of natural balcony formed by the truncated spurs. I reluctantly turned around, returning at the end of summer when the mountain grasses had bathed the slopes in a warm orange glow.

Compared with the long slog up through the forest taken by other walkers, this upper route forces you to gaze *down* into the valley head and its textbook illustration of glacial geography. There are no less than three cirques or corries poised one above the other. The lowest, blocking the head of the wide u-shaped valley with a characteristic triangle of alluvial fan, is the amphitheatre of the Garbétou cirque. Above that, the cliffs of the second cirque, most of them typical glacial *arêtes,* or knife-edge ridges, encircle the étang du Garbet. A lip of rock conceals the water until you are almost upon it, although the water's roar as it tips over the rim marks its presence. Looking up it's possible to make out a third, miniature version of all of this: another cirque with another lake – étang Bleu – that lies suspended yet hidden above.

When I finally arrived at the étang du Garbet, it was early enough in the day for the lake to be in full sun, throwing up a reflection of the surrounding ridges and peaks that wavered little from the motion of ripples cast by a single fishing line. It wasn't until a young woman wearing a white bikini dived into the image that it became fractured. Yet by the time I was walking back the sun had passed over and the dense shadow cast a dark and sinister feel to the valley head. Thinking back to Piston and his charges, they would have had to negotiate their way up here under nightfall, with whatever belongings they were carrying, and then continue along a route that

Couserans doorways

The village of Goutets up on the summer pastures

Above: Mont Béas, above Étang de Lers
Below: The chapel at Le Port

Above: Jean-Marie Claustre's sign and notebook, Mont Ceint
Below: Bilingual street sign, Ercé

Above: Vulture circling above the Col de Pause
Below: The road going up to Spain from the Col de Pause

Above: Étang du Garbet, part of the route used by Piston
Below: Étang d'Arreau with Mont Valier on the right

Above: The long ridge up to Pic Rouge de Bassiès
Below: Looking towards the cirque de Cagateille and the
Spanish frontier at Port de Couillac

Above: Saint-Girons and the river Salat
Below: Market day at Mirepoix

became ever more strenuous, continuing to the frontier at the Port de Montecourbas, where they would descend into Spain.

The first time I'd walked along this section of the escape route, I'd been puzzled by some red graffiti on the rocks here and there; *P 1943,* and, at one point, *Piston 1943,* along with an arrow, in large red letters on a rock. Now I understood that this was someone's attempt to mark the route and highlight its wartime significance with reference to the *passeur.* It seemed surprising that, to date, there was little obvious commemoration apart from an informal and casual attempt using red paint, and it was poorly signposted, with only a few markers and the odd cairn to show the way. Might the entire route ever be promoted as another freedom trail – Piston's path? It felt unlikely. The latter portion from here up to the frontier is probably too dangerous for all but the most experienced mountain hikers.

Every time I walked there I couldn't help remembering one of Scott Goodall's stories as told by Lancaster Bomber Fred Greenwell, who'd escaped to Spain via this route. Among the civilian escapees were a Polish man and his teenage daughter who were finding it difficult to keep up, weighed down by a heavy suitcase. When faced with crossing a raging torrent, presumably the Garbet, the father threw the suitcase down into the ravine to give them a better chance, but the daughter, scared rigid, refused to budge. Eventually the *passeur* escorted them back down to an undocumented fate. Of course this is simply one story among many; evaders did not always make it into Spain, with so many caught by the enemy or simply not having the strength to go on, but I found myself remembering this story every time I walked the Garbet valley. It was the thought of getting that far along a journey of desperation and hope for a future, and then having to live with the decision to turn around, for however long you had left in the world.

And who knew what had been in that suitcase, carried wearily for perhaps months, just to be jettisoned in a futile attempt to keep up.

Despite the decades of emigration and dwindling population from this part of the Couserans, the family names seen on the lists of those deported, killed or aiding in the raid on Ezes were still the same ones adorning the post boxes nailed to the gates of so many of the houses around. So any continuing remembrance would clearly resonate with local families who had a direct connection with the events of the war. Yet I had also noticed that commemorative activities had significance on a broader, more general level with the public. Claustre's hand-made sign on the summit of Mont Ceint might give the impression that he made the climb alone to relive his memories, but in fact there was significant local appreciation of the wartime contribution from that barefoot teenage shepherd. Well into his eighties, Claustre continued to accompany hiking groups, pointing out the huts and *mazucs* he'd used all those years ago and encouraging acknowledgement of the passeurs and their helpers. A report of the trek he accompanied along Piston's route tells how the hikers stopped to read aloud from accounts of the ambush of Piston's group in 1943.[21] And the hikers were not just older people who might have remembered the war; there were plenty of younger faces present, which indicated a rising interest among the younger generations.

I had a feeling that much of this was a reaction to what was happening in other parts of France, and indeed the world. Sometimes we try to make sense of current events by relating them to the past. An account[22] of another Claustre-led walk ends with an acknowledgement that although Nazism and Stalinism are gone, the latest enemy – capitalism – is causing

---

21 http://lesmontagnardstarasconnais.com/120909.htm
22 http://lesmontagnardstarasconnais.com/120528.htm

global suffering. Another wartime crosser of the Pyrenees – the German Jewish philosopher Walter Benjamin – was quoted to tie up the ends by reminding us of his call for people to "defeat capitalism by walking". It was therefore surprising to hear that Claustre's ugly yet poignant sign had been removed in the autumn of 2017 as it was deemed an environmental hazard. Local press reports showed Claustre holding the retrieved sign, claiming defeat by the ecologists but adding a face-saving claim that at 88 he was too old to continue the ascents anyway. Face to face with the unimpressive cairn that had been erected where the old plastic sign had stood, I felt sadness on behalf of the old man. Someone had made the effort to start building a summit cairn, and it wouldn't have taken much more to replace the plastic with a more natural, permanent reminder.

PIC ROUGE DE BASSIÈS

That was as far as I walked in the steps of Piston and his escapees. Driving home from my trek along that part of the route, I pulled off the side of the road at the Col d'Agnes for a last look at the land that Claustre had surveyed to do his bit for the resistance. The succession of cirques at Garbet were darkened and yielding nothing but shadow, and the chain of peaks were in silhouette – all apart from a smooth golden dome rising above the jagged black ridge. It was Pic Rouge de Bassiès, a bulge on the horizon that the sun illuminated with a last burst of gold as it slid behind the chain to the west. Its distinctive profile popped up everywhere I went. Rising up smoothly on one side, the dome breaks off abruptly on the other where its eastern side has been chiselled away, no doubt by long-ago ice action. Walking through the woods in winter, I'd spotted it on the horizon rearing up in white like a petrified breaking wave, the only hint that there was a mountain chain there at all. At 2676m it was higher than anything else I'd reached apart from Mont Valier, but it wasn't a technical climb, just a very long ridge walk that included the exposed section where I'd previously lost my nerve.

The ridges, summits and paths were all beginning to fit together like a 3D jigsaw as I began to realise that today's route offered an easier way up to the mountain, one that would avoid the unnerving section. It would still be a long day, but I knew that I could do it if I really tried. From then on it felt like the mountain was taunting me every time I glanced at it: *still here, see?* Climbers preparing for an attempt on Everest acclimatise by getting closer in stages; walking to a camp, retreating, then walking further the next time and so on. I followed a similar pattern, getting further and further up the long ridge on increasingly longer day walks. Finally, one autumn day I sat at the foot of the dome, wondering if I was really pushing it to climb the final 200m of height and get down before dark. I knew that a lot of it had to do with mindset, and I'd passed a few hikers energetically making their way down, feeling awkward and clumsy in comparison as I moved out of their way. I'd also passed an older couple sunning themselves on a slope above the path and had asked them if they'd been to the summit. 'Non,' they smiled, it was too late in the day. Nonetheless another couple overtook me while I was dithering, and I watched the woman take her partner's rucksack while he slipped off to make a solitary summit bid.

Disappointed with myself, I turned around to descend and was startled to find myself face to face with a large bank of cloud that had crept up silently behind me. It had been hovering for most of the day over the plains stretching towards Toulouse, seemingly stationary. Clearly it had decided to get a move on. Within minutes I was walking through its fine haze and I looked behind to see that the summit was now completely veiled by the cloud. The male walker emerged from the mists, running to rejoin his partner to retrace their steps. The cloud thinned as it passed by, but it remained in some of the ravines and gullies where the ridge dropped away vertically, its white drapes giving an eerie sensation of void just a few steps away. In the middle distance it brought some of the tooth-like pyramidal peaks out of hiding and into sharp perspective as black silhouettes against the shifting cloud.

Back down on the path above the Garbet, the valley was beginning to darken but the early evening golden light held fast on the upper slopes. It was one of those times when an appreciation of the moment comes vividly into focus and holds fast within memory. My walking had become trance-like, an automation induced by eight hours of determined striding, and I was aware that this is a time when accidents can happen. One slip and I'd be rolling down towards the Garbet, and not even the narrow ledge of Piston's path below would be enough to stop me. I sat down on a boulder that radiated the day's warmth, draining the last of my now-cold coffee. The thud of footsteps alerted me to the couple making their way down behind me, and I pulled my legs to the side as they edged past. No words were needed and the smile we exchanged said everything – yes, the disappointment of turning back, but above all an acknowledgement of the moment: being there, in that place, at that time.

TREADING ON MY TOES

'I think a lot of work goes on here on the black. I'm sure some of the French do it and that's probably what some of the Brits do. They come out and they just get by and if that's what you want, then it's fine. But if you want a certain standard you've got to pay for it.' Emma and Mitch had come out a few years ago with the promise of internet-based work for Emma, but this had recently fallen through and the couple were in the difficult situation of living in France without an income. Many of their belongings were up for sale as they prepared to return to England, although the prospect of actually selling the house wasn't looking good. Mitch put it down to the financial crisis and that now people were "wanting more for their money", which meant that houses in the middle bracket, like theirs, weren't selling. 'The house next door has been up for sale for five years. There's one further down the road that's been for sale ever since we moved here.'

We were sitting around a table in what Mitch had pointed out was their "beautiful south-facing terraced garden", although it was also surprisingly noisy. Facing south meant it sat above the main road and the noise from traffic was constant. There was also a rear garden, a large expanse of lawn that had to be mowed using a sit-down mower. The garden was clearly a jewel in their crown as well as something of an irritation, with Mitch using it to show off what they'd achieved: 'It was very, very run down when we got it, the gardens and all the grounds. It's taken two years to get it to looking something like it is now. But that's probably something you'd warn people about if they were thinking of coming over.'

'Don't buy anything with land,' nodded Emma.

'It sounds very romantic, having a place with 2 acres of grounds, but forget it,' said Mitch. 'You're buying hard work.'

Unlike some of the others who'd bought a house out here without having visited France, Emma and Mitch had been familiar with the Ariège, having visited English friends who'd already moved down here. They became tempted to follow as a way to escape from a hectic life in the UK, with Mitch ready to take early retirement. 'We just really appreciated the quality of life that we thought we were going to get by moving away from the hustle and bustle of the UK,' explained Emma. 'We both had quite stressful jobs and we embraced the French attitude, where the family comes first.'

I quickly picked up that Mitch and Emma were keen to distance themselves from the way that other Brits did things out here, going into detail about how they themselves had managed their move. 'One thing we decided was we wanted to do it properly and we wanted to be above board,' said Emma. But according to Mitch, doing everything right hadn't quite worked in their favour.

'I think with us, doing it absolutely the right way, being straight down the line and signed up for everything, we probably lost out,' said Mitch. He sounded resentful of the Brits who stayed outside the French system, owning property in France without becoming full residents. He referred to them as people who come out and play it both ways. 'I think most of the English people we know have still got bank accounts and all that stuff in England. They're people who really want to pretend they're still English and live in England, but they stop all the year out here in France.' Unlike him and Emma, such people had it easier, not having to suffer the French bureaucracy. And why should the Brits benefit from the European health system when they weren't working? 'It's a sort of problem. It's the wrong way to do it – to me, you either live here or you don't.'

It was the same argument raised by John, and although I could see why they felt resentment at the easier life of the "part-timers", I wondered if it was generated more by envy than by anything that was genuinely immoral. In Mitch's case I guessed that some resentment was rooted in the fact that they could no longer afford to live "properly" in France. 'If we'd have done it the other way, on the black, we'd have probably been a lot better off.'

Working on the "black" was not confined to the Brits in France, as the odd French person was similarly to be found supplementing their benefits with a bit of building work here and there. I'd also overheard conversations about occasional odd-jobbing among the English-speaking community, although this was as much to steer clear of entanglement with the terrible French bureaucracy as to avoid paying taxes. The French journalist Fralon, however, claimed that *Handyman for British renovation projects* was one of the three main professions available to the Britons in France. According to him, in some popular regions there existed complete teams of British house renovators. These presented an entire package *au noir*, from the plumber to the stonemason and the roofer, with the advantage of being able to discuss it all in English. The other two professions he cited were as a chef for foreigners, and the ubiquitous English-speaking estate agent, both of whom I'd come across here in the Ariège, although I would also add gîte-owner to the list.

The importance of coming across as the right kind of British incomer was a key theme that afternoon, just as it had been with Pat and John. The conversation shifted to how the Brits should embrace the rules and regulations when moving to a new country. Mitch was strong in his attitudes, referring to the migration situation back in England to make his point that migrants shouldn't stick together. 'In England we call them ghettoes, don't we, when you get all the Caribbean people living here and all the Polish people living there, or whatever,' he said, drawing his finger across the table. In his view it was all wrong. 'That shouldn't be. It shouldn't be in England and it shouldn't be out here.' As always, people were referring to somewhere else in France, not here. Apparently all the Brits were living in the Tarn, according to Mitch, who referred to it as "Great Britarn". And as Mike had insisted, it wasn't only British incomers, was it? 'You've got all the Dutch living in Carla Bayle and so on.'

I'd already come across the Brits abroad using the word *ghetto* to discriminate against each other, but it seemed a vast overstatement here in the Ariège countryside. British clustering was a long way from the forced minority settlements of history, such as the Warsaw ghetto. I even cringed when people used it to refer to the large, purpose-built *urbanizaciones* that were popular with the Brits on the Spanish Costas. So why did it occur in over ten percent of the British press articles that I'd read concerning the Britons in France?

Looking closely at its use, I guessed it was just another flippant comment that followed the stereotype without bothering to think too deeply about it. I'd read quotes in the media from incomers in France who "tried very hard not to fall into a British ghetto"[23], and there were references to Brits living "in British ghettoes surrounded by British mates"[24] or "stuck in a cosy ghetto, watching re-runs of Little Britain". One confusing article claimed the Brits "form ghettoes and buy isolated properties"[25]. Heaven forbid that someone might want to catch up on news back in Britain, since being spotted purchasing a British newspaper "branded" the buyer as "belonging to the British ghetto"[26].

What to make of it all? I had a hunch that there was not much substance behind any of this labelling. The "little England" town of Eymet in the Périgord, where supposedly more than half of the population are English, is perhaps the closest thing to a ghetto, supporting an English chip shop,

23   *The great escape?* The Sunday Express, July 10 2005.
24   *Beware of smug expats,* The Sunday Times, October 15 2006.
25   *Beware of the pitfalls as you break for the border,* The Times, October 13 2007.
26   *Writing my own journal,* The Independent, May 4 2009.

optician and cricket club. But it was also driven by myth. Fralon claimed to have heard a Parisian state that Eymet is so English that they drive on the left, yet, after spending a few winter days there, he concluded that the English residents he came across were pretty discreet and unassuming. A few of them had even picked up the distinctive accent of the south-west of France.

Just as the word *invasion* is frequently used in reports of the British influx, the word *ghetto* is another metaphor that over-exaggerates what it represents. The actual ghettoes were suitably vague, leaving the reader to build on their own assumptions about the way the English live in France. This was the root of the trouble; by presenting these English-speaking ghettoes in a de facto way, the reader isn't invited to agree or disagree; they are expected to simply take it in. And on and on it goes. When people asked me what my research was about, they invariably nodded and used similar language: "Oh I know, they all live there in their ghettoes, and they don't integrate" was a typical response. But no one ever named a person or place where they had experienced this kind of behaviour; it was just reeled off as common knowledge.

Back in the beautiful south-facing garden I was starting to feel uncomfortably hot, and I fought an urge to make a banal comment about mad dogs and Englishmen. The bottle of red wine that I'd brought them as a thank you had been left on the table to boil and I took advantage of a lull in the conversation to quietly move it into the shade.

Despite agreement that the Ariège was distant, both literally and metaphorically, from the sausage stalls and bowling greens of *Dordogneshire*, it was clear that even here the English incomers attached a symbolism to certain actions that showed they were doing things the right way. One of these was the transfer of the car to a French registration plate, which was a sign that you were here for good; not a tourist and not just playing at living in France. I'd already heard Pat and John quickly justify their lack of options in this respect, presumably in case I made an assumption about them not being committed, with John quick to draw a line between themselves and those others "who don't really live here". Mitch similarly drew on this symbol of commitment, showing particular irritation at seeing the British cars lined up at Carcassonne airport. 'Jesus, I hate that. Obviously means they've still got a base in England.' He was quick to set himself apart from these others. 'One of the first things we did was put the car onto French plates.'

'That's a real sign, then, is it, that you're living here?' I asked.

'Absolutely,' he nodded. 'Anyway, I hope we haven't trodden on your toes with some of the comments about how the British are when they live out here.' I looked at him enquiringly. 'I hope we haven't offended you,' he explained, 'by going on about the part-timers.' I felt slightly taken aback. Perhaps I'd been naive to see myself as an Ariège-dwelling insider, admittedly part-time, anticipating that it would encourage people to open up. I'd been aware that I might be seen as the "other" because I was a researcher, but I wasn't expecting to be positioned outside a different kind of boundary – that between the "proper" full-timer and the uncommitted part-timer. Our shared context had felt pretty solid, on the whole. More than one interview had ended with an invitation to return for an evening or a meal out. I shared a love of walking in the Pyrenees with many of the incomers, and our conversations often digressed into an exchange of ideas about different walks. Mitch and I had talked about the routes up close to Mont Valier, and I'd encouraged others to visit the summer pasture huts and *orries* up at Goutets. Many times I'd felt that I was meeting acquaintances rather than interviewing participants, so this metaphorical shove to the other side made me feel a bit dislocated.

Being a proper full-timer also meant using the French rather than the English community. 'We've never used an English tradesman while we've been here, have we?' said Mitch. 'Everything we've had has been through the French.' But this wasn't easy with limited competence in French. Emma talked about the language barrier holding them back socially, admitting 'I haven't got enough French to hold a conversation. If we could speak fluently and get by we'd have a whale of a time.'

But Mitch disagreed that it was down to language. 'We're not stand-offish with the people, but even if the French was very good, we still wouldn't be going visiting French people. In England we had a very good social life and we just accepted that we were coming and that was going to change, and we're quite happy with that change,' he asserted. 'So it's not through lack of choice that we don't go and socialise more and don't go out for meals with people.'

'I don't know,' said Emma, who seemed keener to pin responsibility onto their lack of French. Admittedly it didn't make sense to talk about having an enjoyable social life in England and to then refer to an almost deliberate avoidance of everyone.

'We don't mix with the English very much so we don't mix with the French very much,' said Mitch. 'Just boring, aren't we, really,' he laughed.

I guessed there was more to it than what he was prepared to admit. Aware of the negative stereotypes of the Brits in France, he would have been unwilling to come across as a monolingual Brit, unable to socialise with the French. It was easier to present it as a conscious decision, a choice, that they were coming to France and they were going to be boring and that was that. It was similar to Iris' claim that they hadn't made any effort with the local French.

What gave it away was Emma's admittance that the language was a barrier. To her, it was more acceptable to blame their lack of language skills, rather than be seen as the kind of incomers who deliberately isolate themselves. Whichever way they represented it to me, it was hard to deny that they were so wary of being part of an English-speaking network that they preferred to give up on having a social life. Better to become "boring" than rely on the other Brits around.

A similar thing happened when they talked about the Ariège forum for English-speaking incomers, which they'd used extensively. Emma described it as "like a little comfort zone", although the couple disagreed on their reasons for using it, with Mitch insisting that the internet had taken over and that it was just easier for everyone to buy, sell and find out things online. Whereas Emma acknowledged that they used the English forum because using the French version was beyond their ability. 'You should still integrate,' she said. 'We'll be honest, Mitch, we haven't gone on the French forums to sell stuff because we can't speak the language. So we use the local network purely for that reason.' Again, the lack of language was presented as the factor that steered their actions, rather than a deliberate desire to rely on the English community.

I was seeing a clear pattern among the attitudes shown towards the rest of the English community. Speak French, integrate socially, don't depend on the other Brits. Today there was even a parallel with the situation back in the UK, with Mitch comparing the migrant "ghettoes" in England with the Brits in France.

People had often asked me what the French themselves thought about the English "invasion", and it was difficult to say beyond anecdotes; a couple of people had commented about post office staff being unfriendly towards them because they were English, but that was all. Yet there had been reports of French annoyance in areas such as Brittany; moreover, a French researcher had noted that incomers were being blamed for a kind of fragmentation of the village as a social space; people lived individually, buying houses as commodities rather than passing them down as family homes. But this was surely happening everywhere, not just in France. Moreover, things were very different in the Ariège, where decades of depopulation had left houses and entire hamlets to decay.

Driving home along the snaking valley road, I tried to envisage a future where the English incomers of the Ariège Pyrenees morphed into a more individual oddity, rather like the isolated Welsh-speaking communities in Patagonia. People found these historical migrants interesting, and they aroused curiosity as something unexpected, whereas the Brits in France were something to grumble about. They were much more familiar to us; we watched them on TV, read their exploits in books and there was always that couple down the road who'd made the move. I drifted off into a fantasy whereby the British stopped coming to France for whatever reason, and those who had rooted here among the foothills of the Pyrenees became a rare anthropological curiosity.

THE HALF-BAKED DREAM

The idea of selling up and moving abroad for a better life was thrust into our minds by the weekend supplements, the endless re-runs of *A Place in the Sun* and the neighbours or friends who'd made the plunge to sell up and go. So many people saw it as their dream, their goal, yet it wasn't really a surprise that many of the Britons who'd moved to France found the reality of the new life rather different from what they had imagined. This had been a familiar theme in many of the British press articles that I'd read, and although the word "dream" had often cropped up, it was often used to comment about the imaginings that led people to move to France without always knowing what (or even where!) they were coming to. Writers described it as a "distortion between dreams and reality", and they emphasised that contrast using language such as *harsh truths, wake-up call for Brits, the dream has been ruined, no one can live a dream for ever,* a dream *turning sour* or *into a nightmare,* and even *a half-baked dream.*

Admittedly some of this was blamed on the financial crisis of 2007 onwards, with the weakening of the pound making France rather pricey for those who'd arrived relying on pensions or income in sterling. But there was also a suggestion that the move took place without properly thinking things through. Back in 2010 I'd become curious overhearing the conversation of a family sitting across from us in a restaurant in Cahors, and had managed to strike up a conversation with them. It turned out that they'd read an article in a Sunday broadsheet about buying in France, and the very next week they'd flown out to purchase what turned out to be a serious renovation project. Although the house was close by, they were spending their last night in a hotel, as they'd had enough of holidaying in a wreck. Apparently the floor had given way that week. While the father was still smiling and insisting that they would "be living here" within a couple of years, the teenage daughter sat there shaking her head, muttering "never", while the mother looked on wearily.

I often wondered what became of them. They seemed to me to personify the *half-baked dream* of buying on a whim. Much of what Tina said had echoed this, especially when she talked about being inspired by the writing of Peter Mayle.

Even Gerald talked about "taking the plunge" and buying in an area he didn't know. As a French observer of the English incomers in and around the Périgord, Fralon concluded that what was driving many incomers was a nostalgic affection for the less-populated England of the past, an England that they saw mirrored in the rural France of today. Ariège certainly seems to fit these pull factors: plenty of authentic countryside that's not dominated by everyone else fleeing the towns and cities, and a house that's not overlooked but close enough to a village. If these are people's priorities then it would certainly account for the baffling decision to move to a country that one isn't very familiar with.

What also made sense was Fralon's distinction between the way the English see the British countryside – something precious and rare and therefore costly – with how the French themselves largely view the vast spaces of the *hexagone* as a place for the less successful, the marginals and the excluded – the complete opposite of the British middle-class aspiration. It might come as a bit of a shock to some of the Britons to find that they were sharing one of the most socially deprived départements with some of the country's poorest inhabitants.

This was raised by Mitch in his next point. 'Something we have noticed since we've been here is the decline in social habits, such as the amount of graffiti that you find,' said Mitch. 'And there are more reported house and car break-ins. One young American girl was attacked by the bridge in town, and we've noticed the amount of rubbish that just gets thrown at the side of the river bank.' So they were starting to be aware of the less idyllic aspects, although he presented it as a very recent phenomenon that was "creeping down" from the big northern cities. 'It wasn't happening when we first came out,' he claimed, 'so we've seen a decline in the habits of people in the few years we've been here.'

Emma nodded, keen to show that it wasn't just an English trait to moan about deteriorating habits. 'Even the French people have said they've noticed a difference in town over the last 3 or 4 years. It used to have its streets cleaned regularly and that's all gone, but now the dog mess is terrible. There are certain streets where you're walking like this, hopping on one foot. And the flowers on the roundabouts have gone. I know it sounds silly, but the French go on about it.'

Mitch and Emma had at least been familiar with the Ariège, but it was their keenness to do everything the right way which had partly been their undoing. Privately I wondered whether they would have been better off if they'd stayed as UK residents, at least initially to try things out, rather than registering Emma as self-employed and paying the crippling taxes that France bestows on micro-enterprises. But they also exemplified how easy it was to be influenced by getting value for money and ending up with a house and grounds that were impractical for their needs. Despite the couple having viewed a number of properties, when they actually came to purchasing this house, it was done in an instant – and by just one of them. Emma explained. 'Sometimes your heart rules your head. Mitch bought this house without me even seeing it.'

'Really?'

'Yes, he flew out on the Monday and it was a done deal and he flew back on the Tuesday and that was it. He said *I like it and I've put an offer in and it's been accepted*. I didn't see it until I signed the final papers. I couldn't say no.'

Mitch was quick to remind me that they'd ended up with "a lovely house", but the undercurrent of their impending departure and the reason why – basically that they could no longer afford it – had cast a shadow over our pleasant chat on the south-facing terrace. He repeated that he would warn others not to run away with the idea of buying more than they needed. 'Prospective buyers should think about how they're going to get older, not younger.'

'I think with hindsight we could have bought something smaller, more contained. We might not have found ourselves in the position we're in now,' said Emma. I winced as they said the amount of money they were likely to lose on the house, even if it sold. But things could be worse, they assured me; they had the safety net of a house in the UK that was being rented out, compared with some friends nearby who really were in dire straits. This was a couple who'd bought two properties to renovate and sell on, in what they'd imagined would be a cycle of profitable retirement activity. But now they were stuck with two houses that they couldn't sell and with all their money used up on expensive renovations. 'They haven't got any prospect of going back to England but they can't afford to stay. They're frightened because they haven't got any money to see them through retirement.'

Emma's theory was that France was too difficult for what she called "the middle people", and it mirrored Tina's frustration at being one of those who needed to work, compared with incomers in comfortable retirement or those prepared to live in a shack. But it was as if there should be something in place to prop them up. 'There doesn't seem to be any compensation for people that are prepared to work,' complained Emma. The word "compensation" made it sound as if one was entitled to a reward for taking the plunge: *we've come here, we want to work but our French isn't good enough, so we need something to compensate.* I tried to imagine one of Mitch's Polish migrants saying something similar out loud in an English pub, and the kind of reaction they'd get.

4

THE QUALITY STREET GANG

WORZEL GUMMIDGE IN A JAEGER SUIT

My eyes followed the white-heeled sandals as they flipped up and down between the coffee table and the kitchen, bringing in tea, milk and fresh cookies still warm from the oven. When a second cup was called for, Elaine called to her partner Colin to make it and bring it to us. It was unusual to be sitting inside, as up until now the default setting had been around a table in a garden or courtyard. Today, however, a light drizzle obscured the view out through the French windows. I leaned back on the patterned sofa and admired the cookies, feeling as if I'd been transported into an English seaside town.

'We haven't got a French house,' said Elaine as she set down an Earl Grey teabag for me. 'That sort doesn't appeal to us, a dark old French house. And I've transferred a lot of my furniture here because we couldn't afford to buy new, so nothing in the house is French.'

Once again, it was finding the right house that had governed a move to the Ariège. The couple had crisscrossed France over twenty-odd years, looking for where they might want to live eventually. Elaine admitted that they hadn't known anything about the Ariège beforehand. 'I saw this house on the internet but Colin said *I'm not going there, it's near mountains, it'll be too cold.* So we looked near Mirepoix and we just couldn't get what we wanted for the money that we had. And then we saw this house again, in the estate agent's window in Mirepoix. I said *It's there, look, that's the house and it's a lot cheaper than it was.* I told the estate agent when we were having coffee, I said *That's the one I really want,* and I kept going on about it until he took us so I could get it out of my system. And we walked in the gate there and just fell in love with it.'

Just like Iris and Jim, the choice boiled down to *where the house was.* There was no mention of checking that they liked the village itself, and that it had everything they'd need in their retirement; it was the image of the house exterior that had drawn Elaine. Nothing too exotic, not dark and French, but something that felt familiar. If Kate Fox had tilted her anthropologist's ear over our conversation, she would have nodded and smiled at this evidence that to the English, their home was more than their castle; it was their identity, their status and their prime obsession. It also supported her claim of an all-important English desire for privacy, whereby people like Elaine, and Iris and Jim, base their search on the house itself, trying to find something that isn't overlooked. The town or village, the region and even the country might be almost irrelevant. 'This house is half the size of our house in England, but the gardens are 4–5 times bigger. Now we've got gardens all the way round,' she said. Elaine admitted that they wouldn't have been able to afford that kind of thing in the UK.

With Colin out of the way in the kitchen, Elaine began to open up about how they didn't share the same vision. 'It's my fault, in a way, that we're in France because I gave him the tape of *A Year in Provence* to listen to on the way to work, and he fell in love with the idea. He wanted to be that man with the millstone table.' She'd clearly reflected on how to cope with it all. 'Right from the start, this is Colin's dream, to live here. It's not my dream, it's my adventure.' In other words, she was facing up to it as a practical challenge, something to get through. And as the afternoon went on, it became clear that she wasn't the kind of person to drift through retirement.

Elaine's tendency to organise everyone and everything permeated the conversation. I heard how she'd organised impromptu sightseeing when on holiday in Russia and Morocco, taking groups of women around the resort with her. She'd been mentioned by almost all of the other Brits I spoke to, as someone who organised various gatherings, who did charity work and would be "really good to speak to". People told me that they met so and so "through Elaine". I'd suggested to one woman that Elaine sounded like a kind of hub for the British community, and she agreed, adding, 'Oh yes, and we're all satellites going around her.' Elaine shook her head at this and laughed in denial, although she went on to describe herself in a similar way.

'Yes, I'm quite organised and *I* am the organiser here at home, everything revolves around me. And I like networking. That hasn't changed as I still network with an English women's group.' A few years later, back in Devon, I'd been chatting over the wall to my neighbour's visitors, a couple who'd previously lived in the Aude, and I was astounded to hear that even they remembered Elaine from a brief encounter in Toulouse.

One of the main challenges that appeared to bug Elaine was the financial constraint of living in France on retirement pensions, but as with everything she'd organised a plan. 'Before we came we weren't used to economising, but we did practise living on the limited income that we were going to have on our early retirement pensions. We did that for about 18 months before we came, and found it worked ok.' But they'd still had to change how they lived, and she complained about the novelty of having to save up if they wanted to eat out. 'Money's tight. Every week you cross something off the list. *I don't want that this week.*'

The contrast between Elaine's former life and living here in the Pyrenean foothills was considerable but I was impressed by how hard she was working to adapt, finding numerous ways to use her skills in the new environment. Everything was thought through. 'I still need something to motivate me, I still need targets. I'm a list-maker. I need to achieve every day and at the moment I'm interested in getting to know Toulouse really well. I go to Toulouse at least once a month with an English-speaking guide.' She admitted that not knowing French had put a big barrier in the way of everything. 'I like to build relationships. I like people to know me, the person, but when you can't speak the language there's a barrier there. But I've used different tools to make sure they know that I'm not just that silly English woman who's an immigrant and can't even speak the language.' Elaine and Colin had been to the same French classes that others had described and had similarly given up; not only because they didn't learn anything, but as a former professional, she'd felt highly frustrated by the poorly organised classes.

Elaine described the Ariège people as "lovely" and the culture as "nice", with the lack of commercialism being part of the area's allure. 'They don't know how to market things or present things. Last weekend it was the village fête and everywhere was busy, but the bar was closed, so we went to the *créperie* and it was closed. Closed on a Saturday!'

I asked if there was a specific time that she'd felt particularly foreign. 'There was, actually, when we went to vote in the regional elections,' Elaine said thoughtfully. Unlike Pat and John, who'd told me about getting a "round of applause for voting" as if they had celebrity status, Elaine's experience showed how unfamiliarity with the system could be unnerving. 'It was most peculiar, we sort of stood there for a while as we didn't really know how their system worked. We didn't know how many people to vote for, whether it was 2, 3, 4. I still can't remember what we did,' she mused. 'They tried to explain to us what to do but they couldn't come near us at first. It's all secret, you see. I said *I need aider. Help me, I need some help.*

Despite not really speaking French, Elaine felt that she was "slowly getting there", and much of what she talked about showed that she was active with both the French and English communities. She mentioned a local elderly woman who'd knocked on their door when they first arrived and taken them to all the village dances and festivals. 'She's a very good friend now and I've volunteered to go and help with her garden.' I asked her if she agreed with the sentiment I'd heard among some of the incomers, that actually being competent in French was less important than making the effort. She nodded. 'I don't think it's important and I think it puts a lot of people off from coming. But I still hanker after speaking English.'

Like Iris, Elaine was one of the few who admitted to enjoying the company of the other English speakers, clearly feeling much more at home with them compared with Tina, who had positioned herself as not quite fitting in. I delved deeper into what she felt she shared with them, guessing that she would be honest about it. She listed books and cooking and a shared interest in what was happening in the UK, but unlike Tina, who stratified the Brits into different categories, Elaine drew attention to what she saw as a more level playing field here in France. 'Here we're all in the same boat. We're all expats, we've all got the same problems and difficulties and I don't find that it's competitive here.'

It was interesting how Elaine used different terms to refer to herself. Here, when talking about the shared context of the Brits and their solidarity, they were *all expats*. Yet earlier, when voicing the French who might see her as "that silly English woman who can't even speak the language", she used the word *immigrant*. It was down to what linguists call semantics, where words become "flavoured" by their associations. Academics refer to it as a double standard, whereby it is fine to be an *expat*, that relatively wealthy kind of incomer who could be left to sort things out among their compatriots and not be a burden. But if you were the more troublesome kind of incomer, then you were a *migrant* or *immigrant*. I'd already noted that the British press often used the word *migrant* to distinguish the recent British incomers – who were also *a swelling army, a deluge, a wave* – from the more established and permanent-sounding *residents*.

The double standard of *expat* versus *migrant* has been discussed by migration researchers who claim that it all comes down to privilege. The white Western expat generally enjoys more freedom to settle abroad without any expectation to assimilate, and they are grudgingly tolerated because they have some perceived right to be there, compared with the darker skinned or eastern European-accented *migrant*s. It's true that the latter are never referred to as *expats*. Yet even academics can fall into the stereotyping trap; one migration professor claimed that Europeans living abroad "love to call themselves *expats*", describing them as "haughty" migrants who are exempt from demands to learn the language and do not bother to integrate.[27] It was the kind of lazy comment that strangers said to me when they heard what I was researching, repeating the same old cliché when it happened to fit their own views.

---

27   http://heindehaas.blogspot.co.uk/2015/05/expats.html

Because it was becoming clear to me that, in reality, away from the broad brush of generalisation, things were different. While the term *expat* was certainly used, it was ridiculous to say that it was the preferred term among incomers. If anything, people were aware that it carried a negative association, especially in the British press, where I'd seen writers try to distance themselves from the other "expat types". Gerald too had used the term when distancing himself from the other Brits, referring to what he saw as a more superficial migration of those who *depend for a social life on fellow expats* here in France, as well as in Spain *where they form communities of expats where they speak exclusively English*. Again, the word reflected a sense of entitlement and privilege, a leftover from colonial times that was to be avoided. Another incomer had insisted to me that she was, and always would be, an *immigrant*, and she'd made a point of using the term on the forum when she asked *what other immigrants get up to here*. So at least here in Ariège there were incomers who did not love to call themselves expats.

Expats, migrants or immigrants, Elaine then went on to present the English in a very uniform way. 'All the English are good cooks. And all the English people tend to dress very well.' I raised my eyebrows doubtfully at both suggestions of collective distinctiveness, since I was an example of neither. Perhaps Elaine saw my disbelief as a reflection on her own image, since she went on to add, 'I don't dress quite like I used to. I dress down here because I'm always up on a ladder, I'm like Worzel Gummidge. But I've still got my Jaeger suits that I will not give up for anything. I've just had them all cleaned. Any opportunity to wear them, I'm thrilled to put them on.'

I found it hard to think of many occasions in the rural Ariège when one would have an opportunity to wear that kind of outfit without being extremely conspicuous. Had she done any work apart from charity volunteering? 'No,' she said, 'but I'd love to work over here, on a little job of some kind. I wouldn't mind cleaning and I don't mind cooking and I'm interested in doing some house-sitting. But I have chickens, which are a great bind. It's like having children; we have to get babysitters before we go anywhere.' I had a fleeting image of Elaine bending to scatter chicken feed in a suit and heels.

Just as everyone I spoke to mentioned Elaine, the Ariège English Speaking Women's Group had also been brought up by many of the Brits whom I spoke with. Although everyone spoke positively of Elaine, the Women's Group seemed to polarise people. Some were disdainful, such as Tina who described how members 'sit and discuss how they're going to plant their bulbs, and they have coffee and tea and all those sort of things,' she said. 'But I'm not that old.' Gerald used it as a springboard to be scathing about the more arrogant Brits, claiming that he'd been put off by a few overly critical members who spoke little French and blamed the organiser for everything. 'They'd never offer to do it themselves, not even a lunch, but always glad to criticise others.' But he'd been careful not to over generalise, saying 'they're not all like that, of course.' Now Elaine was describing the group as "stimulating" and a good way to meet English people.

'It's been a joy really, they're very supportive people,' she said. In fact, every one of Elaine's references to the English incomers was at the positive end of the scale. A couple nearby were described as having been tremendous friends to her and Colin. 'I go up once a week just for an hour to speak French together, and it turns into about two hours. She corrects me, she's very good at French.' Another English woman had been their "rock" because 'she knows the French system; she helped us with our first tax form, things like that.' An English builder and his family were "lovely people". Gerald was 'brilliant, he's one of our friends, we call ourselves the Quality Street Gang.'

Also "brilliant" were a family that Elaine and Colin had invited over after the family had introduced themselves on the forum, saying that they didn't know many people. 'They advertised for friends,' laughed Elaine, acknowledging the slightly bizarre nature of the situation. 'They just said *We've moved here but we've got no friends*. I emailed them and I said we're not that far away, so if you get that bored and you want to talk to some old folk, then come and see us.'

I perked up at this as I'd been keen to speak with a family. Perhaps Elaine would be a way in to them. 'I'd quite like to interview them,' I said. Elaine, ever the organiser, leapt in and worked out the process. 'I'll email your email to them. That's it, that's what I need to do.'

It was interesting how complete strangers went online and announced their desire to network with each other simply through the shared context of being English incomers. People had been playing down the fact that they generally all knew each other, not wanting to be seen as part of the English clique, but I'd seen for myself how the forum was used by newcomers to promote opportunities for friendship. One newcomer announced that they were *a couple with a 4-year-old daughter and would love to meet couples, families etc, anybody!!* Two people living nearby gave their email addresses and invited them to get in touch, while another gave out her phone number, stating that she would *love to meet up with a new family to swap stories with*.

On the surface this all contradicted anthropologist Kate Fox's portrayal of the English as reluctant to socialise with strangers outside the home. But of course things were very different here in France, where the incomers had not only left their close friends behind, but they were living among foreigners. Clearly, to some of these forum members, a complete stranger who also happened to be English was preferable to checking out your local network, seeking that all-important shared context and mother tongue. All of this was important to Elaine at the wider level of organising the English-speaking groups, but answering the family's plea on the forum had given her an opportunity to organise things at a more intimate level, coming to the aid of others by offering friendship if they were "that bored" and had nothing better to do. And not only did she step in to offer companionship to the family, but she also came to my aid as she organised my own introduction to them.

I couldn't help but admire Elaine. She'd left a house she loved and enjoyable work to follow her husband's dream, turning it into an adventure that she was working through in her own way. There was no sense of resentment, just a constant aim to adapt to the new context in ways that matched her skills and personality. With her organising of the other Brits and her Jaeger suits, Elaine might have provided ammunition for people who complained about the Brits in France not adapting to the new life and clinging to symbols of the old one, but to me she showed much resourcefulness in adjusting her strengths to what was available. In spite of the very vocal sniping among the Brits about too much dependency on English speakers, many of them nevertheless maintained links with each other. Elaine was just more open about it.

Elaine saw me out and nodded to the man going into his house across the road. 'I can make myself understood now. People listen to me, they're very patient. When we first came here, our neighbour there, Bernard, he was quite disdainful about us and the fact we couldn't speak very much French, but now he appreciates that we're trying.' She gestured to the green lawn. 'Look at that. It's taken a lot of work to get that, a proper green lawn.' She then pointed out the terraced vegetable plots on the steep slope. 'We love what we've got and we love how we've done it. But it's a constant battle of the weeds because it wants to be a meadow. My allotment in the UK was pristine, I mean *pristine*.' The next comment hinted that she saw their future here in the Ariège. 'There's no way we'll be able to walk up that slope when we're older. I've already said, we'll have to dig up the garden to grow our veg.'

Overlooked by the damply forested Pyrenean foothills, Elaine's terraced garden bore no resemblance to the one that Colin had heard described on his way to work, the one with the millstone table, surrounded by a Provençal vineyard. Yet she seemed contented with what they had. 'It's nice living here. We've sort of integrated a little bit into the community, and the English Speaking Women's Group has really been a joy.'

We gazed up at the green forested hills, with the peaks of the Pyrenees changing shape as they appeared every now and then through the low clouds. 'If you want to be part of the smart set you don't come to the Ariège. It's not the Cheshire set here. But the Ariège is what it is. You'll never change the Ariège people and they are so nice, aren't they, in their own little way? Simple folk.'

As I drove away, I pondered that final comment, as it suggested that Elaine would always see herself as an outsider in a land that felt far removed from 21st-century Britain. Ariège definitely lagged behind in the race for consumerism and commercialisation, but changes were apparent, and certainly some of these would have been welcomed by the small influx of foreigners as well as the French second home owners. Even the more alternative incomers expect a decent wifi signal as they rant against McDonald's and disposable nappies. And Juliette's refusal to have a computer in the house, to protect her children from modern obsessions, rang a bit hollow when the children knocked on my door every night to use my mobile broadband to scroll through images of pouting teens on Facebook. The more she resented the school's expectation of using the internet for homework, the more the children resented her refusal to move with the times. As the daughter said, affronted, 'Even the kids living wild up at Ezes have the internet.'

TALK POLITELY TO THE BEAR

Like other mountain regions, the Ariège Pyrenees are renowned for some spectacular waterfalls. Elaine had recommended a gently rising hike along the GR10 to the cascade d'Arcouzan, a waterfall that makes a spectacular 50-metre plunge down from the east face of Mont Valier, and after our conversation I headed out along the track. The ability to stand right beneath the base of the fall made this, to me, more outstanding than another, more famous Ariège waterfall: the Cascade d'Ars, charmingly named after the river Ars/Arse that flows down from the frontier chain and joins the Garbet near the town of Aulus les Bains.

Popular with families and their dogs slogging their way up the forest trail, the Cascade d'Ars, with its three successive drops over 246 metres, is one of the closest things that Ariège has to a tourist honeypot. The following day I set out on a much more engaging circular walk that takes in the isolated étang de Guzet. Climbing steeply up through the woods, I almost failed to spot the tiny green-blue lake just visible through the trees and dropped down to sit at the water's edge, thinking I was alone until I caught sight of red among the rocks. It was another lone woman whom I guessed was also marvelling at the unbroken reflection that spanned the lake, beginning and ending with the encircling ridge of beech trees and rising in the centre to the twin-clawed summit of Pic de Crabe. Regaining the trail and emerging above the tree line, I wondered who had draped the string of prayer flags around a lone hut perched on a grassy ledge. As I stood looking at it, a couple with two dogs stepped out and closed the door, setting off on the path back down towards the lake.

The rock-strewn path became more tiresome as it skirted the flank of the great Mont Rouge, cutting across avalanche corridors that were scarred with rubble. It was a relief to reach the head of the Ars valley where the bulk of another giant, Pic de Puntussan, loomed over the metal bridge across the river. Anchored deep within my thoughts, I was startled by a loud thump and a splash from a boy throwing boulders from the bridge, watched indulgently by his mother. As she packed up their picnic I nipped past them, wanting to prolong the sense of having the mountain to myself. His cries continued to punctuate the roar of the waterfalls long after I'd left them behind.

Mindful of the failing light, I stopped only once, to examine a small metal square printed with a red bear outline. After a fleeting sense of alarm that it was a warning of bear country, I laughed as I remembered that it was one of the signs that differentiated the various walks up to the waterfalls: blue for easy, red for moderate, black for longer and so on. But the existence of bears around here was not a figment of an overactive imagination.

Bears have a long history in the Pyrenees, and in two Couserans valleys they made a significant contribution to the economy. From the late 18th century until the First World War, bear training was a key profession in the Ustou and Garbet valleys, with a bear-training school established in the village of Ercé. All of this is memorialised with some pride in the village's museum of bear training, where the trainers are celebrated as courageous men who escaped their overpopulated valley to make their living across the globe, accompanied by their trained bears.

More recently, bears have been the cause of passionate and sometimes violent controversy. The rapid decline of bear numbers from the mid 20th century led environmentalists to call for a halt to the extinction of this indigenous animal. In 1996 a bear reintroduction programme commenced in the Pyrenees, turning to Slovenia for a supply of genetically close brown bears. At the time of writing there are no surviving native Pyrenean bears, but the bear population of the central Pyrenees, which includes both France and Spain, is certainly growing. The Slovenian bears have multiplied to a relatively young and heavily monitored population that numbered around 39 by the end of 2017. Interested followers can monitor the movement of named bears, such as the lumbering Moonboots, by observing footage from remote cameras of the bears rubbing their backs against the trees. One way of estimating where the bears will be is by monitoring the acorn harvests, meaning that in a good year you might want to be extra vigilant in the higher oak forests that bears tend to favour.

The programme was controversial from the start. The farmers' argument was that too much had changed in recent years to make it a simple process of reintroduction. Not all shepherds live among their sheep on the summer pastures, it being more common to drive up on quad bikes or in 4×4s, but of course this leaves the sheep vulnerable to bear attacks. Resistance from the shepherds has been met with offers of compensation for damages to livestock, and grants to install both electric fencing and a traditional Pyrenean sheepdog – a *Patou* – to guard the livestock. Yet the majority of shepherds continue to protest at what they see as a threat to their livelihood. Anyone driving or walking the back roads could not fail to notice the anti-bear graffiti, with *Non aux ours* frequently spray-painted across the tarmac.

On the other side are the ecologists and the locals who welcome the rewilding. One argument is that the threat has been exaggerated, with protesters using the bear as a scapegoat for all of the other mountain perils. *Pays de l'Ours-Adet*, a pro-bear association bearing a cartoon logo of a smiling bear, claims that the bears' role in livestock destruction is nothing compared with mortality caused by diseases, storms and stray dogs, and especially that other Pyrenean pest, the wild boar. But what about the risk to humans? *Adet* plays this down too, stating that bears are "not particularly dangerous", and although they will approach habitations at night time, they will flee any perceived human presence.

The mayor of Massat has thrown his support behind *Adet* by labelling his area as *commune du pays de l'ours* (a bear country commune). Judging from the anti-bear graffiti on the roads, this isn't a sentiment shared by all inhabitants. The *Adet* website makes light of any danger by recalling the advice once given to children: if you meet a bear, you should avoid annoying it by talking to it politely. I suppose it helps if you recognise which bear it is and remember to use the polite "vous" form: *Bonjour Moonboots! Comment allez-vous?*

These days, hikers encountering the animal are advised to depart quietly without signs of aggression, and above all to avoid the temptation to break into a run. In fact, visual sightings are rare. Out of 1055 presence indicators in the French Pyrenees during 2016, the most numerous type was that of bear hair (380), while discreetly placed remote cameras accounted for 228 sightings. Other indicators were bear dung, tracks or prints, but there were just 18 face-to-face encounters. One group of hikers on their lunch break watched a mother with her three cubs in the Couflens region, and another group in October observed a bear at 30–40m near Aulus. If any members of the public are sufficiently interested or concerned, they are able to consult a regularly updated online spreadsheet showing bear presence indicators by date and commune.

Yet all is not well in bear country, with a mounting assertion that bears and modern farming are incompatible. Parallel with the increase in bear population is, sadly, a growing number of attacks on livestock, particularly in the Ariège, which has become the *département* most affected by bear attacks. 124 of the total (158) attacks in the Pyrenees during 2016 took place here. These attacks have been seized by the press as well as users of social media, with images of ripped-apart livestock shared across sites. All of this has been fuelling the debate to high levels of emotion.

The conflict between the farmers and the bear enthusiasts worsened even further in 2017, partly flamed by one particularly shocking incident. A flock from Couflens that was grazing high up close to the Spanish frontier went into panic when one of the lambs was killed by a bear; the consequent stampede led 208 of them to plummet to their death in Spain. The fact that so many French sheep ended up dead in a neighbouring country made it sound even worse; chased not only over a cliff, but into another country. No one appears to have witnessed the actual stampede, but the link was made when the corpse of the lamb was discovered upstream. According to Steve Cracknell,[28] who spoke with one of the owners at a meeting to discuss the problem, the financial loss is bad enough, but slaughter on this kind of scale involves a loss of decades of selective breeding, since the livestock have built up knowledge of the mountainside that's been passed down through generations.

---

28 http://www.pyreneanway.com/2017/12/rewilding-pyre-
nees-news-about-bears/?lang=en

The anger climaxed in August 2017 after yet another Ariège incident. Thirty or so protestors turned up, masked and armed, to threaten the state experts who had come to assess the damage. The argument made by the protesting shepherds was that they now had no choice but to respond with threats and violence; the menace of the bears meant that they were no longer able to carry out their occupation in a peaceful manner.

At the time of writing the situation remains volatile. Despite armed shepherds threatening government experts who come to assess incidents, the programme continues. The option of a kind of separated coexistence is being mooted as one way forward, despite little idea of how it might work in practice.

JUST A STEPPING STONE

True to her word, Elaine contacted the brilliant family, who with some discernible reluctance agreed that I could come over and talk to them at the only time that they were available – 9am that Friday. It was a novelty to set the alarm and get up in the dark, driving before the sun had found its way into the narrow Couserans valleys. It was also unusual to sit formally around a table inside the dark interior. Not only did it feel more like an interview than any of the other chats, but I felt that I was the one being interrogated by the pair facing me across the table. The atmosphere was guarded, as if Carol and Ray were suspicious about the whole thing. I probably wouldn't even be sitting here if it hadn't been for Elaine's intervention.

In all of the other interviews with couples, I'd sat there patiently while they competed to get their words in, talking over each other and often disagreeing. But at first these two barely moved beyond one-liners, batting just a few words back and forth and agreeing with each other. I knew there wouldn't be an invitation to try their spaghetti Bolognese, nor to join them at the best pizza place in town.

One of the first things they did was to try and place me socially, doubtless because they were aware that I came from a valley that had a reputation for free and easy growing of cannabis. 'I think over at Massat you have smoking parties, don't you?' asked Ray.

'Smoking parties!' I laughed.

'Yes, in the Massat valley,' added Carol. I conceded that some locals might have been growing the stuff as part of their alternative lifestyle, although privately I neither knew nor cared. I went on to describe the yurt building enterprise and Ray was scornful.

'Building yurts – what, as a business venture? Have they got vehicular access?' Not exactly. I explained the scramble up the mountainside and the basic facilities on arrival. Ray shook his head. 'There's getting back to nature and getting back to the Stone Age.' I smiled and added that they nevertheless had a steady stream of visitors. 'Are they druggies?' laughed Ray.

'Now now,' admonished Carol, 'you're making assumptions about the Massat valley.'

'But they're all hippies there!' said Ray. I didn't see much point in correcting him.

Ray began to open up when I asked how they saw themselves in five years' time. 'I doubt we'll be here,' he said. 'Ariège was never a long-term move; it's just a stepping stone. France wasn't my first choice.' This surprised me. Where would he have preferred? 'Far East, Canada, anywhere where there were more opportunities really, but we came here as Carol has family back in the UK.'

So they'd wanted to make a move somewhere, but not especially to this corner of France, or even Europe. So why make a move in the first place? 'We decided there's got to be more to life than just seeing the kids for two weeks at Christmas and two weeks in the summer,' he explained.

I still didn't really understand why they'd ended up here, and it turned out that their primary focus had been buying a business. They'd seen a tourism business up for sale and so the family had ended up here by chance. In terms of practicality it seemed both logical and illogical. In Ray's view, Ariège provided an easier starting point to prepare them for more complicated moves in the future, a gentle way in to becoming a globally mobile family. 'Now we won't be fazed going anywhere else. At any time we can think we've had enough, let's pack up and go somewhere else. It's a stepping stone for the kids too, to be fluent in French and English, you can go anywhere. Next one's Mandarin, I think.'

On the other hand I was finding it difficult to see how this remote département could be a rational choice for a family with no real yearning to be living in France, especially when Carol described herself as "brain dead" nowadays. 'I've gone from a full-on job using my brain cells, and I get here and I don't feel I've got any brain cells anymore. There's also a lack of control because of the language. I feel a lot more vulnerable here than I did in the UK.'

The couple had come out relying on Ray's school-level French, but after having a couple of attempts at lessons, they'd given up, because "real life gets in the way". Carol insisted that they hadn't used that as an excuse to be isolated. 'The key is getting involved. All the way down the line we've got involved with village life, even when we weren't speaking French at the beginning.' But they didn't seem to socialise much, and like some of the others they pinned that on the way they were, rather than any language barrier. 'Even in the UK we didn't have many friends. We just do our own thing, what we want, when we want.'

I wondered what kind of contact they had with other Britons. 'We don't, do we?' replied Ray.

'Well, only those that we've sort of come across,' added Carol. Yet they knew enough for Ray to give a scathing impersonation of British ignorance in the face of his own knowledge.

'The Brits want nannying a lot more here,' he said. 'I asked Sue and John, who went back after being here 6 months, "Have you got your carte vitale sorted?" *What's a carte vitale?*'

He carried on mimicking the Brits, using a slow monotone to portray the cluelessness of their replies. 'It's like Bill and Ben down the road. "Have you got your carte vitale?" *What's one of them?* "Have you sorted your insurance, 'cause if you build a house you're legally required to have it insured." *Oh are we?*'

Ray and Carol made it clear that they weren't like these others. Instead they'd utilised professionals so that everything related to the move was "done properly". I knew that they'd used the British forums, asking questions about English-speaking services and generally advertising their presence, but they were circumspect about it. 'I know of them, yeah,' said Ray. 'But I don't go on them, to be honest.'

'We've occasionally put questions on asking about doctors and dentists and stuff like that,' added Carol, 'but I've not been on them lately.' There was no mention of what Elaine had perceived as advertising for friends.

They were also careful to show that they appreciated the un-Dordogne-like character of the Ariège, where according to Ray, one in four inhabitants was English. 'So you might as well stay in England,' said Carol.

I asked if they'd recommend the Ariège to British people.

Carol laughed. 'Probably not, otherwise it'll end up like the Dordogne and that's when it'll lose its charm.'

Ray was more cautious about encouraging the Brits. 'It depends. The trouble is a lot of Brits come and they expect to be sitting around all day drinking red wine until sundown. And real life isn't like that. Bills have got to be paid, you've got to get in the healthcare system, blah blah blah.' It was the familiar contradiction between the dream and reality; people's expectations versus what actually transpired. Running a tourist accommodation business, Ray had seen his fair share of holidaymakers wanting to uproot and live here. 'They come out with rose-tinted glasses. They come out in holiday mode and then when real life hits them in the face, it isn't easy.'

The silences began to lengthen and I started to make a move, thanking them for their time. Through the window, the sun was just starting to lighten up the valley. Carol looked across. 'When the sun's out it's absolutely gorgeous. It's not so pleasant when it rains, and the winters are bleak. When we first arrived one of the women in the village, who speaks fluent English, said that even for the French, the test is to survive three winters here. If you do that, then you'll stay. We've come through our third winter, so we'll see.'

Winter in the Pyrenees, where temperatures drop well below zero and the snow can fall for days on end, would certainly be a test for the English incomers, even though we're used to moaning about the weather. According to Fralon, it was experiencing the first Dordogne winter that sent around one in six of the new arrivals scurrying back to England in their first year. Realising that they'd come to live in a village that hibernated for half the year, the Brits missed the pubs, the shops and the ability to communicate with more than a handful of compatriots. I expect that many former professionals, like Carol, would have longed for at least a few elements of their previous hectic but meaningful existence, just enough to tilt back a work–life balance that had gone slightly too far the other way.

The following year, when I sat chatting with Lynn, I asked if she'd seen much of Ray and Carol. 'Oh no,' she said, 'they've sold the business and bought one in the Dordogne instead. They missed being around English people.'

THE LANGUAGE PROBLEM

It could have been a flippant, throwaway comment, but Ray's claim that "real life gets in the way" of learning French summed up a particular attitude towards the relative importance of being able to communicate in the local language. The incomers whom I'd met were a mixed bunch in terms of language skills; some came out speaking virtually no French, a few couples managed with one competent partner, and a handful were at intermediate or advanced level. Yet on the forum I'd noticed an assumption that the task of gaining competency in French would largely begin on arrival. It wasn't a total reinforcement of the stereotype that the Brits are largely monolingual, but it didn't fully contradict it either. Newcomers were advised by forum members to *speak French – even bad French*. One member brought in an anecdote to warn a newcomer that *some other Brits moved into our village and were not well received as they spoke "no" French. They left after 3 months.*

It's generally accepted that learning a new language as an adult isn't easy, although the reasons for this haven't been fully explained. There's an ongoing debate between academics who view second language acquisition as a cognitive process, one that's specific to the learner, and those who view the social context as a more significant factor in the success of learning a second language. It seems sensible to assume that both factors are at play, and in the case of the latter, the ease of reliance on an existing English-speaking community would explain the lack of progress experienced by some incomers.

Another factor that interested me was that of motivation. Surely this would be a key factor for British incomers in France, since the move was (usually) deliberately chosen and planned, rather than forced; people had opted to leave the UK in search of a life that was better in some way. I wondered if perhaps some of the initial motivating factors, such as the anticipation of becoming part of the French community, had in some cases become disappointments that had gradually killed off the initial motivation. A few people talked about the French being friendly and polite but not really eager to foster deeper friendships with the incomers. Gerald had been an exception, but even he had been gloomy at the fact that he was unable to be completely himself in another language.

The concept of acculturation – whereby incomers adopt the customs, values and behaviour of the host culture – seems very relevant here. Acculturation is a two-way process, with some choice available to the incomer as to what they are prepared to adapt to; Gerald was a good example of this, with his claim to dip in and out of French culture as he pleased. It's never simply a case of culture being imposed by the host, although some governments do attempt to impose it; think of the attempts by the French to outlaw Muslim attire, and the UK government's attempt to assess migrants' knowledge of life in the UK.

In terms of learning French, it's more complicated, since that aspect of acculturation is affected by the degree of social and psychological distance between the English-speaking incomers and their French hosts. I'd seen clear evidence of social distance, where the ready availability of even a slender English-speaking network encouraged people to take the easier option of socialising in their mother tongue. And as I'd noted with Gail, psychological factors related to anxiety could inhibit less confident incomers from opening themselves up to what they saw as ridicule. In consequence, the less contact they have with the French, the less the opportunities for input, which is an important element of language learning.

The online forum was exactly the kind of thing that reinforced social distance between the incomers and the local community, enabling the Brits to "pull up the drawbridge", in the words of Kate Fox, and avoid the ordeal of face-to-face interaction in a foreign language. Even though the original *Life in France, in English* forum had died in 2011, a replacement had been set up in no time.

For some, such as Pat and John, it was sufficient to learn on a need-to-know basis, and they seemed content with the level they'd achieved. In comparison, Elaine, used to being an organiser, must have felt handicapped by the language barrier, admitting that she found the pressure to succeed too much. As for Ray, he surely would have needed a decent level of French to run a business over here, but his relegation of language learning below the priority of "real life" suggested that his motivation was now flying at half-mast. Perhaps it was seen as not really worth his investment, being as France was a mere stepping stone before moving on to more exciting places.

On the other hand, the idea that acculturation is a forced imposition on incomers seems laughable in British migration contexts. If anything, people saw it the other way round. Pat had talked about showing their French friends the delights of English food and the custom of Christmas crackers, all the while making sure that they didn't come across as enforcing English culture on the French. 'That isn't imposing on them, it's just showing them a little different quirk that we have; we're not saying *well, you've got to have crackers from now on.*' She insisted that their love of curry and fish and chips was limited to when they went back to England. 'We love it but we don't want to make it so we have that here, because it's not right.' The avoidance of imposition was right there in the language, in the very denial of *having* to have crackers at Christmas and making fish and chips readily available. It was an idea rooted within colonial times, one that was refusing to die as the Brits flocked to France.

I'd met a researcher who'd studied British incomers on the Algarve who had looked closely at their motivations to learn Portuguese. Although they all paid lip service to the *desirability* of learning the language of the country, their motivation to actually learn it was, on the whole, low, with people claiming that "everyone speaks English". The researcher, Kate Torkington, also drew attention to how the Brits themselves perceived the economic importance of English. English was viewed as the language with status, so people questioned why they would learn Portuguese when there was little value in learning it. One of the mantras that Torkington heard the Brits using was "we bring the money in", showing how conscious they were of having economic power that brought benefits to the region. This, she felt, was used to underpin their monolingualism, as it was simply logical and legitimate to speak English. Once again, it brought to mind sentiments expressed during our colonial activities.

Something approaching this could be seen in areas of France that had received a more substantial influx of British incomers. In Brittany, for example, the promotion of English language practices was creeping into areas where British incomers were seen as boosting the economy as opposed to being a nuisance. A study by French researcher Aude Etrillard noted how French-owned English-speaking services were beginning to target the Brits. There were guides in English that advised on settling in the area, and on opening guest house accommodation and other small businesses. As in the Ariège, some areas of Brittany have suffered depopulation, and the British influx was seen in some quarters as a welcome demographic route to economic growth.

Compared with Brittany, the Ariège incomers don't enjoy the privilege of using English in everyday contexts. Ariège, with its much smaller numbers of British incomers, makes little attempt to accommodate English speakers. Some of the people of working age I spoke with managed to get by with working for the British community; others had found employment as "the English speaker" in the estate agencies. Some had their own property or accommodation services, where they could muddle through in the event of having a French customer. Yet the Ariège promotes itself as a tourist destination, and English is the language of communication for more nationalities than just the British. The Ariège.com website does its bit by having an English version of some of its pages, so acknowledgement of the global economic opportunities related to English is creeping in, but slowly.

THE LEGACY OF VASCONIA

Many of the Britons I spoke with blamed the broad regional accent for not being able to converse well with the local French, complaining that it was so different from the French they'd learned in the classroom. Even Gerald said, 'I can't join in with the patois, I don't understand every word.' Here in the Ariège, people were often surprised to find that one *did* pronounce the final letters of place names. While in the north one would say "Massah" as opposed to sounding the final -t in Massat, here the /t/ was pronounced. Even French radio announcers got it wrong, much to Vincent's amusement, as well as English

161

broadcasters. I smiled at Jasmine Harman guiding viewers around "Massah" during an episode of *A Place in the Sun* and inviting Steve and Lisa to look at properties in the town of "Says". Perhaps the programme producers were aware that the /x/ is pronounced in the name of Seix, and they altered it to avoid it sounding like a place of debauchery. But how many Brits then walked into estate agents asking for properties in "Says"? And even the accepted pronunciation wasn't without its disputes. According to the Gasconha.com site, which promotes the older language of Gascon, a more authentic pronunciation of the /x/ would be as a 'sh' sound, as it would be in Catalan: "Seish".

I'd come to the Ariège aware that there was another, older language spoken here, one that was related to Catalan. I'd begun by thinking of it as "Occitan". I'd been thrilled to see an inscription that was clearly not French – *Enso mieu que soun pla* – carved into the lintel over the front door of a nearby house where, until recently, an old Ariégeois had spent his later years at rest in front of the huge open hearth. This made me smile, since the inscription translated to something like *Home is where I want to be*. But I came to realise that I'd misunderstood the whole conception of the Occitan language, starting from a conversation with an English researcher I met at a linguistics conference. Every time I mentioned Occitan, he shook his head. 'There's not really an Occitan language,' he repeated. 'It's just an umbrella term for a number of different language varieties. I'm studying the Prouvençal variety, but in Ariège you might be talking about Gascon.' He was right.

Nowadays, Occitan isn't just an umbrella term for the languages; it's an entire heritage movement. Growing interest in the old languages has led to a handful of language immersion schools known as *Calandretas* being established, as well as some radio and TV programmes, together with opportunities to learn and study the language in universities such as Toulouse. Yet it was also linked to sociocultural and political aspects as much as the promotion of a tangible Occitan language. The term *Occitan*, or the *lange d'oc*, came into being in the 14th century to differentiate between the languages spoken in the south and the north of France. The *lange d'oc*, spoken where *oc* was the word for *yes*, is a legacy of the region's proximity to Spain and Italy, but just as the researcher had said, Occitan isn't a clearly defined, individual language. There are a number of related varieties within southern France as well as in Spain, Italy and Switzerland. All of them share the same Latin root and some characteristics, but they are nevertheless distinct.

Gascon is one of these varieties. The name originated from Vasconia and the Vascones tribe, who were related to the Basques at the other end of the Pyrenees. Maps of dialect surveys showed a vertical boundary running through Ariège, and I'd heard, anecdotally, that the Col de Port forms a rough demarcation line, with Gascon spoken to the west in an area that corresponded to the Couserans designation. Languedocien is the related variety spoken further east, such as around Mirepoix and Foix. Therefore, despite the apparent logicality of the Occitan movement promoting a regional language known as Occitan, calling it by a single name doesn't make sense to the linguists studying the different varieties. Well-meaning though it is, the profile-raising of a generic Occitan language ignores the distinctive characteristics of varieties such as Gascon and Languedocien.

The variation of the linguistic features across these varieties makes it too simplistic and arbitrary to define one set of parameters as "the Occitan language". To give one example: Gascon sometimes adds an /a/ before an initial /r/, whereby the languedocient *riu* becomes *arriu* in Gascon. To make it even more complicated, Gascon itself can vary across the region since it encompasses a number of dialects such as *béarnaise* and *aranais*, the latter being officially recognised over the border in Spain. This is why it makes more sense to refer to Gascon as a *language variety*, as opposed to a *dialect*.

The number of Gascon speakers has seen a sharp decline over the last 150 years. According to a survey carried out in 1864, over 90% of the Ariège population at that time were speakers of Gascon, rather than French, yet few people speak it now. France has a long history of marginalising its regional languages, and only in 1951 was the teaching of regional languages authorised, under the Deixonne law. In a detailed study by Nicole Marcus,[29] she reveals how some of the older remaining speakers of Gascon had been forbidden to speak it in school and had been humiliated when they did. Not surprisingly, they were reluctant to pass it down to their children. It had become stigmatised as an inferior dialect, with even the speakers themselves referring to it as a patois, not acknowledging that it was a historically distinct language variety.

I'd met a Canadian professor, Penny Eckert, who'd observed this shift from Gascon to French while researching in the Couserans village of Soulan in the early 1970s. Eckert talked about the stigma associated with Gascon, particularly when it was infused with the broader Couserans dialect. Returning to the area in 2005, Eckert found that some villages had completely lost their Gascon speakers, noting how they'd been replaced by incomers from Toulouse, Paris and even England. A few years later our paths crossed at a conference and I introduced myself to her, thinking that we shared some common ground in our research fields. Her face showed a flicker of annoyance when I mentioned the British incomers,

29   http://digitalassets.lib.berkeley.edu/etd/ucb/text/Marcus_berke-ley_0028E_10746.pdf

blaming them for overcrowding the rural areas and polluting the hillsides with their septic tanks. Perhaps she'd encountered a few irritating types, but the population of the hillsides was still only a fraction of what it had been a hundred and fifty years ago.

There were visible traces of Gascon in the Ariège, mostly the odd house name using the word *enso* rather than the French *chez*, as in *Enso Bernard*. Elsewhere one saw few remnants of what had once been spoken by 90% of the population, although I'd noted bilingual street signs in Ercé, a village that leans considerably on its bear-training past. Like most other villages of the Couserans, Ercé had suffered considerably from a rural exodus over decades, going from well over three thousand inhabitants in the 19th century to just five hundred-odd in recent years. Ercé's museum tells of the waves of emigration, beginning with the trainers with their bears who toured the fairs of America during the later 19th century. A second rush took place shortly after the First World War, when Ercé lost around 20% of its population to the US, and a third wave of emigrants left as France recovered from the Second World War. All of this is commemorated in the *Espace des Montreurs d'Ours,* a museum dedicated to the bear trainers.

As the bear training occupation declined, the emigrants took on other kinds of work, particularly in the New York restaurant trade. They would regularly meet up to share news from back home, gathering at a rock in Central Park that became known as the Rock of Ercé. I often thought of the Ercé migrants gathered together around the rock, speaking French no doubt, perhaps with a little Gascon punctuating the conversation, as they exchanged news of the valley. In other words, they would simply be doing what immigrants do everywhere, but here it was an activity that had affectionately moved into legend territory. I wondered what the English incomers, with their insistence on avoiding one's compatriots, would have had to say about it.

Above Ercé lies the hamlet of Cominac, which is another celebrated reminder of Ariège heritage, due to its unusually large collection of picturesque barns that lie scattered around the hamlet. Gazing out from Cominac, one stands face to face with one of the most classic views of the Couserans, seen in books, on map covers, on blogs and tourism websites: the stepped gables of the barns, the green pasture sliced through with a sweep of the road, and the distinctive outline of the Mont Valier massif. Back in the days when the slopes were given over to livestock farming, these clusters of barns meant that there was always hay close by during the winter months. Those around Cominac are noted for their distinctive kind of stepped gable known as *pas de oiseau* (bird steps), a remnant of the former thatched roof that allowed access to the roof whilst also helping to protect the join from wind and rain. The thatch has long since been replaced by slate, which was conveniently mined from local slate quarries from the end of the 18th century. An even earlier form of roofing can be seen around the Couserans; the distinctive half-moon shaped lauzes, carved from slabs of schist.

Some of these old Couserans houses bear reminders of how farming was an integral part of everyday life, making the most of the space and the constraints of the slopes to combine the two. Houses like my own were built into the steep slopes, where the first floor, accessible from behind, could serve as a ground floor for the inhabitants or be used to store hay. The actual ground floor was often used to house cattle or animal hutches, or utilised as a tool shed or for activities such as weaving, basketry and clog making.

It's common to come across isolated stone barns whilst out walking up through the hillside forests. Some of them have fallen into ruin, with roofs long gone and an open doorway or window offering a glimpse of the trees growing up through the interior. A growing number have been renovated for permanent and holiday homes, offering eco-solitude for anyone prepared to haul supplies up through the forest. Whilst walking on the path up to Goutets I'd passed a few where a sleeping bag and even a snowboard glimpsed through the windows suggested occasional habitation. Juliette had admitted that she'd spent the odd day seeking simplicity in some of these barns when the modern trappings of the house became too much for her.

LA SIMPLICITÉ DE LA MONTAGNE

After leaving Ray and Carol I walked back to my car and pulled the bike out of the boot, setting off for the Cirque de Cagateille. This spectacular gouge in the mountainside was another remnant of the ice age, and this autumn its grey walls were spattered by an exceptionally vivid array of bright reds, yellows and oranges from the turning beech woods. It's possible to hike up the side of the cirque, over the lip and onto the edge of a small lake – étang de la Hillette – that was encircled by another wilder rocky amphitheatre that formed the frontier with Spain.

I locked my bike, stepping carefully to avoid a motionless adder that I couldn't be sure was alive or dead, and began the long walk across the valley floor, then climbed steeply over huge flat boulders with thin ridges running the length of them, until I found myself at the glacial moraine that formed the lip at the edge of the lake. Here metal foot rungs had been placed to ease the climb down to the water. The frontier crest looked tantalisingly close – perhaps another hour's walk – but I knew I'd be pushing it that day. Instead I mentally parked it and came back a couple of years later with Terry, who was as excited as I was at the thought of crossing the Pyrenees into Spain on foot. It turned out that distances were deceptive, and what I'd envisaged as perhaps a solid eight-hour walk took us eleven. It was partly the altitude; starting at 900m and going up to 2,450m was considerable height gain. Moreover, what I'd assumed would be a quick descent turned out to be as hard as the ascent. Tiny streams sprung out everywhere and we exhausted ourselves trying to avoid a slip on the smooth faces of the boulders. Night had fallen by the time we made it back, with the canopy of trees blocking out the failing light, causing us to stumble over knotted tree roots that crisscrossed the path. It was a lesson learned and from then on I kept a head torch permanently in the backpack.

When I first started walking alone in the Ariège Pyrenees, I limited myself to easy day walks, happy with simply gazing up at the Pyrenean chain as a backdrop. I'd read all the advice against walking alone, and I was often over-cautious, sometimes spotting an interesting feature or a route on the map but fretting about whether to do it alone. One challenge was to learn and recognise the Pyrenean chain profile from different angles, to name the summits and the notches silhouetted on the skyline. Over the years I ventured higher and higher, until the mountains were no longer just a scenic backdrop, but a relief map dotted with routes and summits that I now recognised. Even a hesitant clamber over the exposed arête of Cabanatous, where I momentarily lost my nerve, was accomplished without mishap, and at the end of the long day I was approached in the car park by a young French couple who said they'd watched me from the lake far below. 'We thought you were very brave,' the woman said. I just nodded and smiled, not letting on that I'd had to give myself a silent talking-to as I sat momentarily frozen on the arête, gazing at my new boots with their fronts badly scuffed from my clumsy scramble.

In the mountains I learned to listen out for silence, and I gradually came to realise that silence in the mountains was a *noise*. I got used to being alone to the point that one day, behind the camera lens after three hours of solitary walking, I jolted at the sound of hoarse breathing, and looked around sharply, expecting to see an animal nearby. It wasn't until I caught sight of a flash of red movement that I realised it was another hiker, a male in a red jacket who was cautiously waving to me, clearly aware that I'd been startled.

That was on the summit of Tuc de la Coume, the moderate peak that I gazed at every day from my window. I'd wanted to climb it for ten years, but the maps showed no direct path, and when I'd tried I'd turned back, defeated by thick bracken. I'd seen photographs of people standing on the top so I knew there was a way up there. In the end a local put me right, telling me it was just a case of getting to the crest of the ridge and then just keeping going. And that was all it took, beating my way through bracken that was beginning to die back in early autumn, and scrambling over rocky outcrops until I finally peered down a drop of 900m to see the windows of my house gazing back at me on the opposite side of the valley.

There on the summit, next to a weathered wooden stake, was a tangible reminder of the sometimes fateful lure of the mountains. Someone had carried up a granite memorial to 'Christian':

Ce qui fait l'attrait et la beauté de la montagne, c'est cette simplicité absolue habillant d'une sobre élégance la pierre nue. Est-ce... pour cela... qu'elle l'appelait et qu'elle le rappela. Toi Christian en ce dimanche 18 mars 2001.

Asking around later, I was told that Christian died when walking below the ridge, beneath an unstable snow cornice. I cleaned away the bird droppings and read it whilst standing on the narrow summit ridge that separated the steep drop behind from the vertical plunge just a few steps in front that fell all the way down to the hamlet of Ezes. I could relate to the epitaph, understanding how someone had come to terms with a tragic accident by accepting that it was all down to the magnetic pull of the mountains, of nature. It wasn't a slip or foolhardiness that had taken Christian; he had merely answered a call – a final summons – from this particular mountain.

MONT VALIER

The GR10, a long-distance path from the Atlantic to the Mediterranean, winds its way across the Ariège département with a number of variants, and many sections afford views of Mont Valier, one of the most well-known peaks of the Ariège at 2,838 metres. Valier gives its name to one of the oldest Nature Reserves in the Pyrenees, one that stretches across 14km along the Spanish frontier. The mountain itself is a significant landmark, up there with the other Ariège jewels of the Cathar site of Montségur and the medieval architecture of Mirepoix. Its distinctive "shoulders" are almost always visible on the horizon. As the English mountaineer Charles Packe wrote in 1867, Valier is so conspicuous from all sides that "it is impossible to persuade the peasants of Ariège that it is not the highest point of the chain." The classic "shouldered" view of Mont Valier also gives sight of the sole glacier of the Ariège Pyrenees, the Arcouzan glacier, which is also one of the smallest at some 370m × 90m. Lying on a barely accessible north-east face at around 2,400m of height, the glacier only began to be scientifically measured in 2011. Nevertheless, it's clear that the Arcouzan glacier has decreased considerably in size over the last century. Unlike some of the other melting glaciers, the shrinkage here is perceived to have stabilised, yielding hope that this distinctive feature of Valier will remain for a while yet.

The summit of Mont Valier itself can be reached via a strenuous but not particularly dangerous route up the Riberot valley, breaking the journey with an overnight stay in the well-known Refuge d'Estagnous before a final ascent of the summit pyramid. This particular refuge had played a crucial role in many of the wartime escapes over the Pyrenees and today it forms a stopping point on the Freedom Route, offering a place to reserve a bunk or even a tent. Visitors can take advantage of experiencing dinner with wine included at a height of 2,246m.

Having seen Mont Valier close up from all sides, Terry and I finally fulfilled our ambition to climb it at the end of the 2015 season, thinking it would be more adventurous to reserve a tent rather than a communal bunk. For some reason we stuck to that decision when we arrived at the refuge, even though we were the only guests. The sleeping mats that the warden handed to us were no match for the damp rocky ground where we set up camp, and we fidgeted through a broken night's sleep that was punctured by the chiming of bells from the cows that lumbered around throughout the night. The cows had already spent much of the evening staring through the window at us while we ate dinner and drank the carafe of wine served by the solitary warden. Our dessert – an unusual fruit compote, like a chunkier version of fruit mincemeat – was presented to us as *old man's marmalade,* so named because the old man "doesn't have a wife".

It's also possible to have a particularly close encounter with Mont Valier without much walking at all. A road starting from

Couflens in the Salat valley goes all the way up to the Col de Pause, which is the end of the road for most drivers, although a track continues to twist its way in a crazy fashion all the way up to the Spanish frontier at the Port d'Aula. Dating back to the 1970s, the road was begun as an attempt to forge closer links with the Spanish, but the Spanish never completed their side. The lower section is generally open through the summer, although it becomes more nerve-wracking as one gets closer to the Col, with much of the road twisting its way around single-track hairpins. There is nothing to stop a car from going over the edge.

I avoided driving up the road completely the first time I visited the Col one August, having seen it featured on a *World's most dangerous roads* website and knowing that the GR10 long-distance footpath runs parallel. I cursed my cautiousness when I finally arrived at the Col to see so many cars parked, especially as I'd missed much of the GR10 signage and had wasted well over an hour retracing my steps here and there, all the time feeling drained by the waves of heat that the road reflected. But the views were spectacular. With each gain of a hundred or so metres of height, the panorama over the Salat valley and the endless line of ridges gradually unfolds in a way that only a walker can truly appreciate.

On foot one can also take time to observe the small villages that the GR10 passes through, yet the only signs of life were seen when negotiating the narrow passageways at Faup, a village perched on a kind of natural balcony above the valley, when I disturbed a late afternoon gathering of locals to ask the whereabouts of a water source. The most spectacularly sited village of all – La Serre – was deserted, the shutters all fastened tight to blank out the vast glacial arena, with its hollowed and folded ridges and cirques, that lay just across the valley.

I returned to the Col again and again that summer. I drove up as far as I dared and sighed with relief when I met nothing more than the odd shepherd out looking for sheep corpses to throw in the back of the van. Driving part of the way up allowed more time to continue walking the GR10 beyond the Col, cutting across the impossibly tight bends of the frontier track to reach the étang d'Arreau, a pea-green jewel of a lake that sparkles and reflects back an almost circular arc of the surrounding peaks. The silence of the mountains was broken only by the involuntary *aah* of the odd hiker as they arrived at the point where their eyes caught sight of the water.

Another time I walked from the Col de Pause up to the summit of Pic de Fonta, a ridge that towers over the Col and yields a panorama of the endless folds and ridges of the Pyrenean chain, as well as the plains running north to Toulouse. On the way back down I was surprised to meet three hikers coming the other way, as it seemed late in the day to be going up. It turned out that they were heading for the GR10 hostel at Rouze, on the opposite side of the valley, having missed the signs for the path at the Col. There was no sign of a map and I had some difficulty persuading them that they were going in the wrong direction, but eventually they believed me. Two of the three decided to cut down the steep slope to the road, visible through the woods far below, while the third hiker, filled with nervous energy, opted to follow me along the path back to the Col, excitedly shouting "GR dix? GR dix?" every couple of minutes. Eventually he left me, running to catch up with the others who'd emerged from the woods. They were already pushing it to get to their destination before dark as they had a steep descent to Couflens followed by an equally steep ascent. But at least they were on the right path now. I don't know where they'd have ended up if I hadn't turned them around.

As I'd sat alone on the upper slopes of the Pic de Fonta, I'd been startled by a rush of air as a pair of wings swooped close by, and looking up, I saw forty or so of them, circling around on the midday thermals. They were griffon vultures, the *vautor fauve* distinguished by their white collar ruff and drooping round head that contrasts with the pale brown of the body and the short dark tail with its fanned-out flight feathers. They continued to circle for the next hour or so, taking advantage of the rising updrafts and thermals to soar around looking for carrion. These carnivorous scavengers had multiplied quite rapidly in France since being endangered in the 1960s, although their numbers were minor compared to the thousands over in Spain.

Here in France there were growing concerns about the increasingly aggressive nature of the vultures. Reports had been coming in that they were turning from scavenger to predator and targeting live animals, not just carrion. Just as with the bears, the conservationists were at odds with the farmers, and here there was an added undercurrent of a potential serious risk to humans. In April 2013 the body of a woman hiker had been found an hour or so after she had fallen whilst walking in the mountains near Larrau. The problem was, the "body" had, in that hour, been stripped of flesh. Only her bones, clothes and shoes lay there; the rest had gone with the vultures.

Some were blaming this increasingly predatory nature on the recent regulations laid down by the EU, who'd ruled that any dead livestock had to be immediately removed, to help control the spread of BSE. Obviously this had had consequences for the growing vulture population, who were now facing stiff competition for food sources. The French Vulture group of the *Ligue pour la Protection des Oiseaux* saw fit to publish, in English, a clarification report against what they termed a distortion of facts by "some media with unscrupulous sensationalism", singling out "the British tabloid press" for its opportunistic blaming of the EU. It was no surprise to find that it was the Daily Mail that had featured a noticeable anti-EU stance when reporting the story.

One of the more ghastly aspects was the possibility that the vultures had begun to gorge before the poor woman had actually died. The ecologists and others dismissed this and insisted that it was simply not possible – vultures don't scavenge on live prey. Nevertheless, there had been some claims by farmers of weakened lambs being taken, so if that was really the case, then why would a vulnerable human be treated differently? The French Vulture group attempted to remind us that what had happened was, however shocking, a natural example of nature's efficiency, which is true. And yet... the fact that farmers were being warned to keep carcasses away from vulnerable live animals and livestock buildings acknowledged that the unspeakable remained a possibility.

5

LIKE A SOAP OPERA

━━━

THEY DON'T KNOW WHERE ELSE TO TURN

'The Brits coming over now, they're not expecting the same thing as we were when we came. It's a shame in a way, and I'm adding to it by selling this stuff,' laughed Felicity as she looked around the shelves stacked with British brands. 'But I do have this side of me that thinks: you're coming to live in another country, you shouldn't expect it to be like it was in England. Surely that's the idea of moving somewhere?'

We were sitting in what was, at that time, another British shop in the Ariège. Felicity was a relative old-timer, having moved to France some twenty years ago with her children, who were now bilingual. Like some of the other incomers, she'd intended on buying in the neighbouring Aude, nearer to Carcassonne, but had "drifted" into Ariège. The area had been familiar to her as she'd spent childhood holidays there.

I'd been particularly keen to speak with Felicity as I was aware that her shop was seen as a central point for the Brits in the area. Iris had commented how much better she felt after meeting Felicity and "the network that she represented", meaning the way that Felicity acted as a knowledge base for the Brits and any problems they experienced. Felicity described herself in similar terms. 'I'm a bit like a drop-in service I suppose,' she admitted, going on to list all the things that she'd been asked to do over the years. 'People come with all sorts of paperwork, *what's this?* and *what does this mean?* and *can you just phone and make me an appointment?* and *I've got this thing...* You wouldn't believe the things I've done for people; reading blood test results, making appointments with specialists, going to hospitals in Toulouse with them for the appointments, you name it. I've translated people's wills and tax returns. It's extraordinary,' she said, nodding at my raised eyebrows, 'but they don't know where else to turn.'

I agreed that it sounded a surprising level of responsibility, but Felicity exuded no sense of resentment. 'This is how it works,' she stated. 'I'm a friendly face and I'm a point of contact and if I can't help then I know somebody who can. And that's why I'm here,' she smiled. 'I'm never going to make myself a fortune by having a place like this. I'm doing it because I absolutely love it.'

What interested me was that although Felicity claimed to love helping the incomers, it was viewed as a vocation rather than a social activity that fulfilled a need to be with other Brits. In fact she was adamant that she didn't actually *socialise* with the other Brits, feeling that she didn't have much in common with them. 'It's difficult, because I do favours for them, they kind of feel they need to pay me back somehow, so they invite me for meals. I find it hard to continually say no,' she laughed, 'so I do socialise in that sense. But having said that, I don't invite them to my house, ever.'

So it was her calling, an accepted responsibility to help out the other Brits because there was no one else, *it's what I'm here for*. At the same time, she acknowledged that it wasn't exactly ideal for people to come over and "muddle through" with their limited French until something happens, when they become "just totally and utterly lost".

Felicity confirmed my belief that people were moving to this corner of France with no French at all. 'Oh definitely,' she nodded. 'They've found an English-speaking lawyer and an English speaker at the bank and an English-speaking estate agent and they think it's going to be as easy as that,' she smiled. She admitted that she'd discouraged some of the dreamers who were under the impression that they could get work anywhere. 'So France, that's already got its own unemployment problem, is going to take your husband, who can't communicate with anybody, over a French man... No, it doesn't work that way.'

I was enjoying how Felicity animatedly voiced the dreamers, raising her eyebrows in mock glee as she mimicked them. '*Ooh, we'll go over and have a gîte*, and then they find that you spend all this money and you get your gîte together and then actually nobody comes and stays in it.' And it was all evidence to support that theme I'd seen in so many articles about the gap between the dream and reality.

Felicity knew of others who'd come to the Ariège with a dream of making a living as a builder, then found that there weren't enough Brits around to keep them in business, since the French largely preferred to use their own established French-speaking compatriots. And then there was that peculiar British phenomenon, the cowboy builder. She told an anecdote about a British builder who'd been sued by some British incomers for a large amount of money. 'He didn't help himself. He went to court for the first proceedings and basically stood up there and said *Je ne pas parle français* and prepared a statement in English, and you think, why on Earth would you do that? You must have some friend or somebody that would go with you.' She shook her head. 'Unfortunately there's a lot of cowboys. I get the stories, *don't go to him, don't let him do your kitchen/ bathroom/extension.*'

This wasn't a problem confined to France, as I knew from my own experience in England, but the English cowboy builder did seem particularly notorious over here. I guessed that the root problem was the same in France as in my home county of Devon: people move to areas with little work, they think about what they can do, and if they have some previous DIY experience then they decide that's enough to become a builder. With so many of the British incomers unable to speak a reasonable level of French, they would have a captive market. On the other hand, unless they'd been there for years, it was unlikely that they would have had a French builder's knowledge of local building techniques and materials, as well as a local builder's links with all of the other craft- and tradespeople in the area. Mitch had been keen to point out that they'd only ever used French tradespeople. But I knew from Mike's regular building work with English incomers, and the frenzy of excitement when a plasterer announced his arrival on the forum, that many of the others were excited at the thought of a tradesperson who could speak their language.

A French customer came in to buy teabags and spent a few minutes chatting with Felicity about the teachers' demonstration taking place in the main square. I took the opportunity to cast my eyes around the shelves stacked with British staples such as tinned soup, sliced bread, teabags and baked beans. One corner was given over to a range of teapots, and an entire shelf was stacked with infant formula. Were the purchasers buying things for a nostalgic indulgence, or did they genuinely feel that British brands were must-haves? Felicity admitted that both kinds of customer came into the shop, although she found it weird to see people get excited about things that they had so far been able to live without.

'They come in, then they see it and they go *ooh, you've got that* and it's all *must have some of that.* But I bet your life they haven't thought about it for months or years.'

Even more bizarre were those for whom the shop was their main source of groceries. 'I've got customers who actually want me to get English-brand tinned peas and carrots. They come in here and treat it as a weekly shop, going *can't you get this?* and *can't you get that?'*

Here, at last, was confirmation of the unadventurous British stereotype living in the Ariège. Nevertheless, it was difficult to ignore the high prices of the goods on the shelves. Felicity read my thoughts. 'Obviously stuff that I'm selling is going to be an awful lot more expensive. Why would you pay twice the price for jam that's come over from England, when it's better in France?' It was a good question, and I had no idea why, when perfectly good French jars could be bought more cheaply.

Felicity's close contact with so many new arrivals, as well as holidaymakers who dreamed of making a move, provided valuable insights into why incomers were choosing the Ariège for a new life in France. She summed it up as there being enough of an English-speaking back-up in a place that still felt like France. Then she shrugged. 'It's one of the last undiscovered places, isn't it, so I think it's probably down to price on the whole.'

Although Felicity's role in helping the Brits was both informal and unpaid, it was clearly defined and I expect that grateful incomers used the shop where possible. There were other areas of France where this had actually developed into a paid job – *aideur d'Anglais* – according to the journalist Fralon. In Limousin and in Dordogne, for example, there were Britons holding down jobs as facilitators of communications between the incomers and the French administrative system.

I'd been struck by Felicity's reluctance to mix socially outside of this role, and I wondered aloud whether she felt different from the rest of them. She frowned, thinking about it. 'Do you mean like the old school and the new arrivals?' she asked, and then nodded. 'I think possibly, yes. Some of the Brits who've come in more recent years do have this expectation that it won't be as foreign, but when we came, you faced the fact that there wasn't going to be anything British.' She pointed to the shelf full of British milk formula that was waiting for a customer. 'There you go, silly things like baby milk, *can you get me in some follow-on baby milk? I can't find the right baby milk.*' She loosened up, voicing comments from customers that she must have heard over the years. '*This is what we know, this is what we like, this is what we need. It's* things like that. It's *yes, we're moving to France, but we want all our things from home around us, we don't want to be that foreign.*'

Felicity then made a point of emphasising that none of this actually bothered her. I understood that she was perhaps mindful that she might come across as being critical of her customers, the people whom she unfailingly helped out. 'I haven't consciously thought of it before, but once you asked the question, then yes, we were the pioneers I guess.'

Of all the people I sat chatting with, Felicity had the most reason to moan about the dependencies and unpreparedness of some of the new arrivals. Yet compared with almost everyone else I'd spoken with, she was careful to avoid drawing boundaries between herself and the other incomers. Even when she admitted to the possibility of feeling different, it was presented as something that emerged only after I'd got her thinking about it. She gave no hint of showing scorn or derision, only of concern for the dreamers.

Even when we moved on to talking about the online forum, her tone was solicitous rather than scornful. I asked her if she found it interesting to read the posts on the forum, wondering whether she'd been intrigued, as I had, by the kinds of questions people had asked. She nodded, saying predictably that she enjoyed helping people and sharing what she knew about life in France. But then her face dropped. 'I do despair though that some of the stuff is so basic, really. *You haven't got a clue, have you?* sort of thing. And that does worry me a lot.'

Felicity was the real thing in terms of support, exuding concern rather than judgement. There was no sense of the other incomers being perceived as sad and wrong, or a "sore point". Even when mimicking their demands, there was no invitation to sneer; that was just how it was.

If I had to give one enduring point from my observation of the English incomers in Ariège, it was how people's attitudes towards behaviour – their own and others' – was overshadowed by a pervasive duty to do things properly, to fall into the category of the "right" kind of English person in France. Almost everyone I spoke to or observed was at pains to demonstrate it. The fact that it raised its head in almost every conversation, on the forum and in so many of the British press articles, showed the extent of the social pressure to be seen to conform.

The online forum was where it was at its most raw, due to the disinhibiting effect of being able to write what you want behind the screen. Recent years have seen a huge rise in trolling on platforms such as Twitter, so much that it's sadly become a feature of everyday life. Yet back in 2007, when the forum infighting was at its peak, it was less common, which made the spate of insults on a supposedly supportive forum even more unexpected. One particular newcomer had been singled out for asking too many simplistic questions. *He comes to France but can't be bothered to get off his backside and explore a bit. Cotton wool has nothing on him.* The insults grew, labelling the new member as *someone who wants help with everything because his mindset tells him he can't... who I think of as a joke,* someone who *obviously needs a bum wiper to survive.* Other members, affronted, waded in to point out that the whole purpose of the forum was to support each other. They questioned why he felt it acceptable to act like this online when surely, if the conversation had taken place in a bar, the person posting the insults would have acted *in a normal, human way.* The moderator took the step of banning the troublemakers but the damage was done. For a new member to be labelled *a joke* really did call into question that person's social value as part of the English-speaking community. In spite of the support rallied from other members, that particular incomer didn't make an appearance on the forum for over a year after this incident, citing the "problems" he'd had before.

The consequence of all of this was that people sometimes had to carry out quite elaborate reasoning to explain their behaviour if it didn't fit that of the ideal British incomer. I'd heard people claiming they had a duty to show the French what the English eat, while others, who were unable to mix with the French and unwilling to network with the British, stated that they were "just boring" people who'd decided not to socialise in France. I didn't find it particularly surprising that people made such effort to avoid coming across as that negative stereotype.

It would be easy to sneer at the incomers as privileged people with the means to leave Britain and buy into a dream life in France, but like any dream, it was vulnerable: to the economy, to exchange rates, to illness and to the uncertainty of political developments such as Brexit. Moreover, life in France could not be divided, in binary terms, into doing things the right or the wrong way: *you either live here or you don't.* In spite of almost everyone denying the existence of a tangible

British community in the Ariège, each and every one of those I spoke with belonged to a definable group of British incomers. Drawing on the stereotypes was an attempt to marginalise people, and it was felt acceptable to do so because the criticisms were aimed at a faceless mass, those other embarrassing Brits elsewhere. It was cliqueyness, but it was something else too; it was attempting to evaluate each other according to a hierarchy of social worth.

JUST A VOYEUR

'One of the things we quite like is the sort of strange mix of people here, because there are some very alternative people and some very respectable-looking people, and they all seem to rub shoulders quite happily most of the time.' Rosie didn't raise her eyebrows when I explained that I was based near Massat, nor did she comment on what a strange place it was.

I'd arrived late at the house of Rosie and Glyn, overheated and apologetic as I confessed that I'd underestimated the time it would take to get there by bike. They'd sent directions but the existence of more than one garage on the route meant that I'd become confused by which one to turn right at. But eventually I found the potholed lane with its 50kph speed limit sign that was, as Rosie said, "a complete joke". Soon thereafter I spotted the British-registered car that was parked at a precarious angle on the almost vertical track leading down to their house.

Rosie and Glyn graciously accepted my apologies, more concerned than annoyed about my breaking the first rule of interviewing – never be late! Glyn made his excuses, leaving me with sun-hatted Rosie to seat ourselves around a table shaded by a kiwi tree. Compared with Elaine's "English house" and

John's "former wreck", this house had barely been renovated or altered by the couple. The floor tiles, the faded paint and the woodwork were all old, the kind of thing that most of the other incomers would have gleefully ripped out and replaced, but I found it charming and of course it was perfectly serviceable. As I made my way though the ground floor to find the bathroom, I sensed the decades of rustic simplicity.

Rosie and her husband had based their decision on where to live with an unusual degree of logic. They'd lived in France in their youth and had family living elsewhere in the country, and had discovered the area whilst on holiday. 'We liked the people. They seemed friendly and more open to people from other places. And we liked the things that went on round here,' said Rosie. 'And of course the walking's wonderful.'

What's more, I thought they'd chosen their house in the best possible way. 'One day we were out walking along the track you came in on and we saw this house down here. We'd seen it in the agents but I'd never been able to place it.' I found it hard not to smile, feeling a sense of appreciation at hearing someone, at last, give a rational reason for choosing their home. It was less a focus on finding the actual house – *where the house was* – and more about what was available in the place where they wanted to be.

I asked Rosie what she thought about people moving here without having visited the area beforehand. 'I've no idea why anyone would do that. It seems very odd to me,' she said. Like me, she found the forum posts interesting to read. 'I'm just a voyeur,' she laughed, 'I can't remember how I found the forum but I was just fascinated. Some people don't seem to have any idea what they're coming to. I did wonder if it's been on a television programme or something,' she mused.

I confessed that my own absorption with the forum had triggered the whole idea of this study. She nodded in understanding. 'It's like a soap opera, isn't it?' she laughed. 'Someone recently asked a question about noisy creatures in the loft, so another member tells them that they're *loirs*, or edible dormice. And the person asking said *oh yes, the neighbours said they thought they were loirs but we weren't sure what they were.* I thought, hold on a minute, you're on the internet, you could have looked it up. I suppose they thought *edible dormouse* was something out of Alice and not real, so they had to ask somebody English to have it confirmed. I thought it was really sweet actually.' She laughed. 'So I think there are whole stories in there, aren't there?' I nodded. There were indeed whole stories to be interpreted from just a simple question and answer. It was a charming anecdote to support the idea of *pulling up the drawbridge* – that the Brits are more reassured by asking each other things, even when a native expert is on hand.

As for *loirs*, they were indeed a noisy menace, and that autumn I'd been kept awake many nights by them running around above my head, playing ball with the nuts and small apples they were hoarding in the enclosed beam space. The couple next door had complained about them when they first moved in, but they'd now moved across into my house. Perhaps they'd been disturbed by Claude's banging and hammering, and the stream of "fucky fuck fuck" when things weren't going so well – all the more startling as it was the only English word I'd ever heard him utter. I didn't fancy my chances with Vincent's blowpipe, as I never actually *saw* any loirs – just heard the racket every night – but eventually I invested in a plug-in ultrasonic rodent remover, and the noise disappeared. I envisioned them decamping back to next door, carrying their apples and nuts.

Like some of the others, Rosie brought up the idea that life in the Ariège was inevitably simpler, comparing it with the UK but also elsewhere in France. Although she had family members living in France, they'd visited and declared the Ariège to be "the back of beyond". 'I think you've got to like a fairly simple life to live here. If you ever get invited into people's houses or peer into them, they haven't got lots of new sofas and things, they've got the French one that was passed down to them. They're not always out buying stuff and all that kind of thing, so it's a much simpler life in material terms.' Nor was it a place for those whose idea of a better life included evening socialising. 'Round here they seem to have a pretty short day; they get up when the sun comes up and more or less go to bed when the sun goes down. The bars here shut at 8 in the evening.'

Rosie and Glyn's experience with the local tourist board provided a neat illustration of the Ariège approach to marketing. 'They have an English version of their website but they were using some automatic translator and it was coming out with utter nonsense; not just bad English, it was nonsense. So we offered to do it, and Glyn sent quite a few pages through but they never did anything with them. So he's given up. Somebody offers you free translation and you don't take it,' she laughed. As I'd noted, the global status of English, and its perceived economic value, had some way to go here in the Ariège. 'These sites need to have proper English, because it's not just for English and American people, is it?' said Rosie. 'It's also for Japanese and other people who use English as an international language. If they have another language here, it seems to be Spanish, which I can understand. But I've been amazed at how few people have wanted to try out their English.'

I asked Rosie whether she knew many other Brits around, and she admitted that she'd come across a few but had not had any contact with them. That wasn't entirely deliberate. 'When we first came I said *I don't want anything to do with English people,* but I've relapsed on that now,' she admitted. 'I just think they're people like any other people. If we meet them, they might be nice, and they might not, and we may have nothing in common.' Rosie and Glyn had seen the brilliant family in the tourist office, noticing how they'd seemed to be struggling with their limited French, and, like me, wondering how they managed with running a business. 'It would be a tremendous disadvantage,' she said. 'I don't know how you'd ever find out what was going on. The local paper's very good but even for us it's quite challenging, as it's always full of acronyms and I've no idea what they are. But for people over here trying to run businesses with no French or very little, I don't know how you do that, because the red tape is massive.'

Both Rosie and Glyn had studied French to degree level and considered themselves to be proficient in the language. But she supported my observation that it wasn't always about the language itself; confidence and personality were also significant factors. I'd noted how Pat and John were confident enough to go to every local event, despite having very basic French, and even when people didn't understand them, it was the fault of the French. Yet Rosie found some situations difficult, not because of the language itself, but more from how she saw herself reflected back in the interaction. 'I'm not very confident. It depends on the person I'm speaking to. As soon as anyone slightly doesn't like me because I'm a foreigner or something then I start stammering and stuttering all over the place, which is crazy.'

I found it interesting that she included being foreign as a possible reason for dislike. It linked back to the idea of identity and how it's a two-way process – not just how we see ourselves, but how we perceive others see us, reflected back as in a mirror. All of this can affect our sense of belonging, self-respect and self-esteem. In foreign-language situations it can be exacerbated, to the point that researchers have termed the phenomenon Foreign Language Anxiety (FLA) – a feeling of tension and apprehension when trying to speak and be understood in another language. For the Brits in France, with that shadow of the stereotype hanging over them, it could go beyond anxiety about simply being understood. Who would want to be seen as the monolingual Brit caricature?

According to academic Dr Gianfranco Conti, it's down to the way that anxiety affects our working memory. When we're working out what to say, we store what we've already said while also processing the next bits. Working memory also plays a role in learning vocabulary, as it notices and encodes new words. Words and sounds are held within our working memory by something called the "phonological loop", but when we get anxious, our inner "thinking" voice takes up too much of our sound storage resources, hampering our ability to store and process what we're hearing.

So I could understand Rosie's reasoning, although whether it was based on a real or imagined dislike of her foreignness was difficult to know. It was nevertheless down to how she perceived herself as being seen, that idea of a mirror in interaction; if you feel others perceive you negatively, you become flustered. I now understood better why my own French turned into rambling repetition when talking to officials or friends, because these were higher-stake situations where I was anxious about not being seen as an idiot, or that *Brits in France* stereotype. Yet the same mediocre French would come to life in random conversations with strangers where I was just a foreigner out for a walk.

I got up to go but sat down again when Rosie invited me to stay for lunch. Glyn had kept out of the way during the interview, but he became much more garrulous once my notebook was out of the way. We sat around the table and chatted like friends as we pored over maps of the area, with them recommending routes around Coumebière, and me pointing out the routes up to Goutets. Eventually I got back on the bike, freewheeling around the potholes back down to the main road where I was grateful for the shaded valley that kept the sun away. It was hotter than ever.

THE ONLINE AMUSEMENT ARCADE

Ever since that first interview with Gerald, I'd been contemplating his idea of a particularly English sense of humour here in France. It wasn't just his claim that the French tend to expect us to be humorous and eccentric, but also the anthropologists' assertion that humour has a central importance when the English interact. Rosie's reference to observing the forum as like watching a soap opera sent me back to it to gauge the centrality of wit in the online interactions. What I found was, indeed, a natural undercurrent of humour throughout the posts.

As in conversation, the English trait of not taking oneself too seriously cropped up, although, as always, not everyone understood the intended irony. One discussion focused on the complications of French bureaucracy when setting up small enterprises, and it invited a comment *At least it keeps the competition to a minimum!!!!* ☺. One member missed the irony and replied, in seriousness, *That might be ok for some people*, so that the original poster felt obliged to explain: *You took me toooooo seriously... I was only having a laugh... no one in their right mind would start up a small business.*

The importance of not taking oneself too seriously was strongly reinforced against one particular forum member who just seemed to be permanently angry. There was no humour in his own rants, but the other members made up for it by drawing on their own wit to deflate his self-importance. He had harangued against what he saw as the British *drop-outs,* claiming that he and his wife *work f***ing hard* at living and working with the French. He'd gone into detail about their struggles, mentioning how they'd worked at cleaning stairs and offices and toilets; they'd done unpaid work experience and at one point one of them had been in a wheelchair. All of this had been addressed to another member – *a sad person who does nothing to move on in life* – whose "crime" was to have merely said how difficult she'd found it to gain employment in the Ariège. The other members replied with irony: *I trust that you do not work in the customer service industry?* as well as a parody of a parody from a classic Monty Python sketch: *Please cease with the "our father used to wake us up an hour before we went to bed and feed us cold gravel for breakfast" routine.* And when the same angry member listed his local involvement and asked what everyone else put back into the community, the immediate response was *Well said, Mother Theresa of Ariège.*

But was all this humour merely a national characteristic of the English, a default mode to be funny and ironic, or was there something else going on? So many examples drew on things that were familiar to people from the UK that I began to see it as a kind of in-group solidarity, using humour to sustain an emotional connection with each other here in France by referring to things that were peculiarly British. A member who'd ranted about French business practices – *the mangy corpse of French retailing* – had subsequently tried to temper his criticism by claiming *I'm not for painting the Ariège B&Q orange either,* a wry metaphor on the homogeneous state of English out-of-town centres. Another member asked about where to buy furniture and received the response *Don't forget*

IKEA down at Toulouse. I know that they're the furniture equivalent of Ryanair (obloquy be upon them). This led to a stream of jokes ranging around English cities: *I get the weirdest feeling when I'm walking round Ikea in Toulouse. After I've been in there about 45 minutes, I swear when I walk through the exit I'm going to find myself in the car park of its Bristol branch.*

The humour continued when the angry member raised his head in yet another criticism of the UKers, stating: *You lot will never learn. If they don't speak English you are all lost sheep in a huge field.* Presumably he saw the references to IKEA as yet more evidence that the Brits were reliant on English-speaking services, despite IKEA being Swedish of course. His comment received the best kind of snub: an almost total disregard apart from one indirect response: *I was in IKEA Bristol on Thursday and noticed everyone was speaking English!* I showed this example of English irony to a French friend, who shook her head, saying 'I don't understand why that's funny.'

Yet the Brits generally avoided using humour on the forum to poke gentle fun at the French. The one extended rant that I saw against French business customs generated a stream of protests from the other members. It started out with black humour about the inability to go shopping during the two-hour midday break: *At 12:00 prompt I would like to be in the car park outside the Carcassonne branch of Darty, whereupon I would hurl a brick through its window. I'd then crunch my way into the shop across the debris, put a couple of batteries in my pocket, slap the money on the counter and crunch out bellowing a cheery "thank you" over my shoulder.* After this exaggerated opening, the member explained the reasoning behind it: *How in the hell can a business afford to keep the lights on with all that working capital on the shelves and human capital on the payroll when willing customers have their noses pressed up against the glass from 12:00 to 14:00?* More criticism followed about the fact that prices were often absent or incorrect. *Where's the bloody manager? What do you do all day apart from prepare for and recover from your two-hour lunch break? Get a bloody clue!!!!*

Despite the attempt to lighten the tirade with sarcasm and hyperbole, the underlying grievance was quickly and firmly stamped upon, with other members unanimous in their support for the French way of life. *I came to the Ariège because it was slow, laid-back… a bit behind the times. I wanted to get away from the mad 24/7 existence I have in the UK.* And if the Brits didn't like it, well, it wasn't down to the French to change, but the incomers: *I MUST LEARN TO CHANGE, I do not want the Ariège to change.* I guessed that people were aware of how easy it was to become hypocritical, something highlighted in the *Britlands of Périgord* by the journalist Fralon, who noted how incomers would claim that they'd left England for the French way of life and the leisurely lunch break, yet still expect a shopkeeper to leave his lunch table and serve them if they were in a hurry.

Gently satirising the French is often seen in the relocation literature, such as Mayle's likening of the Provençal physical welcome to an airport frisking. Yet I came across very little mockery of the French on the forum, and none during my chats with the English. It didn't seem that surprising, since the incomers were only too aware that they were guests of the French. What's more, few would want to be seen as that British stereotype, acting like a colonial, coming in and changing things to suit what they were used to. The very existence of the stereotype is a threat to the incomers, since none of them wants to be aligned to it. It was therefore understandable that humour was used more often to try and neutralise that threat by making fun of the dependent Brits.

A rather different example of forum humour was a spoof post that turned up, written by a supposed "new" member in the guise of a French person:

> My friend jimmy say look at thes site for funny laugh, see what england send to France. I am French, ow did england win 2 wars of world and beeted Napolian when i reeded of people who in Ariege can not the find wood for burning in fire, can not the fire shop to buy the fire discover, can not going to big shop when open buted closed and find the faults with the worker for stopping to eat, know noted how to get electricity, a lady who thinks the anglais will change the ecomomie francais. The man Nick he is funny i lik the person smizz he is crazy idiot. Tell if me why you live en France if so difficulty or you lik to speak of chains for pnues for long time?
> appy christmas et new year
> nichole

It was an attempt at satire by one of the members, and a pretty crude one at that. Whoever wrote it was attempting to come across as a French person who had little control of the English language; someone who didn't understand the irregular past forms of the verbs *beat* and *read*, and couldn't spell them either. Yet their control of written French was similarly poor, misspelling the word for tyres – *pneus* – as *pnues*, as well as making a basic blunder with the spelling *Napolian*. It was a classroom attempt at mockery, with giveaway errors.

I reckoned a more Standard English version would go something like this:

My friend Jimmy told me to look at this site for a laugh, to see what England sends to France. I am French, but how did England win two world wars and beat Napoleon, when I read of people in Ariège who can't find firewood, can't find a shop selling wood burners, who go to superstores when they're closed rather than when they're open and then blame the workers for having a lunch break; people who don't know how to get electricity, and a lady who thinks the English will change the French economy. But Nick is funny and I like Smith, the crazy idiot. Tell me, why do you all live in France if it's all so difficult, and why do you go on and on about snow chains?

Happy Christmas and New Year,
Nicole

The writer was what's now referred to as a "sock puppet", someone who creates a fictional online identity in order to dominate an online discussion, skew the balance of debate and spread fake news, although the intention has also been to promote or criticise a product by writing phony reviews. Researchers are developing ways to detect these kinds of multiple accounts, using analysis of writing style, for example. Back in 2007, it was a startling example to post onto a support forum, but it seems unlikely that the writer was trying to be taken seriously. The errors were more confusing than clever, perhaps as a result of someone having written it in a hurry, without much thought. Yet someone took the trouble to write it, satirising the forum members using insider jokes that only a forum user would understand. For instance, I remembered the online discussions about firewood and buying wood burners, as well as the thread on setting up a micro enterprise in order to obtain health insurance that developed into a critique of the French economy, as well as the rant about the retail park shops shutting at lunchtime. There had also been a very long thread about the necessity to carry snow chains and whether one could buy a set that would fit any hire car.

As a humorous attempt at satire it failed to garner many reactions, and I suspect this was partly due to the effort required to decipher it. Perhaps some members felt it wasn't even worthy of comment. One member made a serious observation that there was no way it was written by a genuine French person with those kinds of deliberate errors. He went on to say that he'd heard similar, if more authentic, comments expressed, so *there might be something in them*. The "funny" member Nick (a pseudonym here) replied to say *who cares, at least it is better reading than chains, fish and chips and the rest of the tat and it happens to be pretty accurate*. Researchers note that one of the giveaways of sock puppetry is the writer's relationship with other users, and this unsubtle example points to the writer's link with the two named members; in fact, he was quite possibly one of them.

Pervasive the humour certainly was, but not all of it was deemed acceptable by the other members. The attack on the newcomer who was likened to cotton wool, who *needed a bum wiper,* had been justified by the writer as *banter that brightens up the otherwise dull and boring website. I like to be sarcastic. Unfortunately most of the Brits leave their sense of humour in Dover.* As other members waded in to protest at this idea of "humour", the forum moderator also reinforced the purpose of the forum as a means of support. *It is not an amusement arcade. The day will not come where I provide cheap entertainment for vulgar individuals.* But even the moderator drew on humour to reinforce his point: *If you want an adventure why not head off to Africa or some snake-infested South American jungle. Maybe then we will be impressed by your survival skills.*

196

It all demonstrated that what Kate Fox called "the most effective built-in antidote to our [English] social dis-ease" – the sheer pervasiveness of humour in English everyday life – didn't get left behind when people moved across the Channel. Humour came as naturally to the Brits online as did the preference to ask each other for advice rather than the local French. Yet it also served to remind them of their shared context, alongside a darker purpose to reinforce that boundary against the more embarrassing newcomers.

THEY ALL GO *QUOI?* AND DO THAT FROWN

'Suddenly I'm in this place where they're not speaking the French I've learned at all and I found it quite depressing to begin with.' Susan and I were sitting around the same café table that I'd sat at with Iris and Jim. I had to work hard at keeping on top of the conversation, as Susan's voice was often drowned out by the lively French customers. Visiting her at her house hadn't been an option; Susan and her partner had bought an isolated barn five years ago, and the focus of the renovation had initially been on creating a garden. Even now they managed without mains water and relied on a generator for electricity.

Susan had studied Open University courses in French before the move, but she'd found her inability to keep up in local conversation a disappointment. The regional accent had been a shock. 'At times I wondered *what have I done this for?*, because learning to speak the language and working towards being fluent was a really important part of coming out here.' Like Rosie, she laid some of the blame at her own shyness, particularly her nervousness when talking to strangers. 'I try and talk to people and I talk quietly because I'm nervous and

they all go *quoi?* and do that frown they do, because they're not
sure what you want from them.' Once again we were coming
back to the anxiety factor, and I couldn't help but notice that
of everyone I spoke to, it was the women, such as Gail, Elaine,
Rosie and Susan, who talked of their concern about coming
across as a silly foreigner, making them inhibited when talking
to the French. Not one of these women lacked motivation to
learn and speak French, but that motivation was affected by
anxiety chipping away at their confidence.

Susan compared her own arrival in the Ariège with that
of another woman who'd now gone back to the UK after
setting up a *chambre d'hote* that didn't work out, and then
found it impossible to find any kind of paying work. 'She came
out with no French at all as far as I can gather; she'd got this
absolutely terrible French, no grammar to speak of at all but
she did it with panache. Everybody seemed to know what she
was talking about,' she laughed. 'Whereas there's me with my
diploma.' She laughed again. 'I don't want to make it sound
as though the woman didn't care, she was trying to improve,
but she'd just got this confident manner and got on better
than I did at the start because of that.' I nodded. I knew what
she meant. Stig and I were at a similar level with our French,
able to hold a conversation, but our walk up to Goutets had
highlighted my own shyness compared with Stig's buoyancy.
I'd noticed how he spoke to every local that we passed, about
the weather, the route and even admiring an elderly lady's new
roof, while I held back, afraid of getting into something that I
couldn't fully understand.

Susan's motivation went well beyond just learning French
to get by. Here was someone for whom conquering the
language had been a fundamental part of the move, not a
by-product of it. Some studies of second language learning
claim that in fact it was *never* just about getting by, but about

becoming the person you wanted to be – the ideal self. For someone like John, who aimed to get by on a "need-to-know basis", that basic level of achievement was sufficient. To him it was pointless to aim for "that mountain you're never going to climb". Susan, on the other hand, had envisaged an ideal self that was fluent and had become disappointed, as had Gerald. Not surprisingly, those who kept their expectations low had less chance of being disappointed. For the Brits in France, I expect it was also about not being seen as that clichéd *Do you speak English?* incomer.

I tried to get to the bottom of how it affected Susan's sense of identity. 'Do you feel different from any other British people here?' I asked.

'A bit,' she admitted. 'Perhaps it's the language thing. I feel different to the bulk of them, I think. I get the feeling that I might speak French just for the sake of speaking another language, whereas for most people it's a means to an end.' She confirmed my thoughts about the gap between anticipation and reality. 'I think maybe I had some unrealistic expectations after doing all that hard work in England, and that in a couple of years I would be totally fluent, it would just flow out of me. But five years on it's just not flowing out. It's not bad, and on a good day it's quite good, but it's not always good.'

It was good enough to help out some of the others. Susan was the "tremendous friend" who was helping Elaine at that time. Chatting with a friend was one thing, but, like Felicity, Susan had been asked to accompany people to doctors and hospital appointments. 'I've done that with two different people and I didn't even feel that confident about what the doctors were saying to me. I had to take it on board and say it in English to the other person.'

I winced. 'That's quite a responsibility.'

'It's horrible actually. I hope nobody ever asks me again.'

Susan and her partner were in early retirement and like Iris and Jim they'd left England for a new challenge in life. 'We felt that life is too easy, we knew how to do things. I mean, we're talking five and a half decades of it. Things looked predictable and we were up for something a bit different.'

'So why did you end up in the Ariège?'

'We spent three months travelling around France in a motorhome and got very familiar with the place,' she replied. 'It always felt very comfortable here in France, it felt like the sort of place you could live.' But they never got as far as exploring the Ariège itself. 'We went to a show about France in Earls Court and we got talking to an estate agent in Saint-Girons and she said *well, you couldn't do better than Ariège, it's beautiful.* And it sort of sold us, so we came back out and had a look and we thought *this is lovely.*'

Susan admitted that she did little socialising and that most of it was with other English people. 'We never set out to do it, it just kind of happened. It's so much easier to chat to somebody in your own language, isn't it? And none of the neighbours have really shown any desire to be best friends. They're perfectly polite, perfectly nice and friendly but it just hasn't happened.' As with some of the others, she claimed that socialising with the community wasn't something she'd anticipated. 'I have to say I'm not a very sociable person. If people aren't around I don't go out and find them.' Yet she relied to some extent on being part of an online community, particularly that facilitated by Twitter. 'There's always someone there to respond to me, however banal the tweet,' she said. 'Without it I'd have gone mad.'

A few people had mentioned Susan and it always revolved around her garden. The other incomers found it intriguing that the garden took precedence over making the barn more habitable. But it was the move itself that triggered the obsession with gardening, as if moving to the Ariège had presented an opportunity to reinvent oneself. I brought in Gerald's concept of *narrenfreiheit*, the foreigner's freedom to be a bit different. Susan nodded enthusiastically, adding that being here was like having a clean page. In the UK everyone knew what to expect of her, but here she could start afresh. 'I've never been the sort of keen gardener I am now,' she admitted. 'I've had little tiny gardens that mostly I didn't do a great deal with, so that side of life is very different now. It's like new work. It's not just a hobby, it's more than that. It's what I do.' They'd taken care to choose an area where a typically English garden wouldn't stand out, avoiding the open area around Cominac, for example. 'The kind of compartmentalised English garden that we planned to make would have been very visible and out-of-place up there.'

As we got up to go, Susan said something that surprised me. 'Actually, I don't feel *completely* settled here. I lack the feeling of having roots like in the UK.' We agreed to keep in touch and a year later we met again, sitting outside a café in a village close to her home. She was full of enthusiasm about the ecological swimming pool they were building, one that filled naturally with rain and was kept clear by carefully chosen plants. As before they were keen to avoid something that didn't sit well within the environment. 'A normal pool would look too out-of-place,' she said. But then the conversation turned back to what she'd expressed in that departing comment last time – a feeling of frustration. 'Sometimes it feels like I'm not *living* in France, just spending time here.' As before, the disappointment was related to language, and a feeling that she'd reached a plateau with learning French. 'I go to the hairdresser and I reckon I understand, properly, only around five per cent of what she says.' Despite all this there was no suggestion of returning to the UK. 'We'll probably stay here in the Ariège,' she said. 'I still feel lucky that we chose to come here.'

Interlude

LUCKY TO BE HERE

————

A couple of years later I was driving back to the Ariège after a winter in England, playing a mental game of *Who will I see first?* Some of the locals were like landmarks to me, and I was like a child, ticking them off as I spotted them after being away. These weren't acquaintances, but people that I always saw around and about, familiar figures in the landscape. There was Black-dog Man, who stood outside his bric-a-brac shop, surveying passers-by and booting his dog when it tried to nibble donkey manure. Waving Catwoman was an elderly lady who stood in the road or crouched at its edge, gesturing at the cars as they drove past. If she wasn't there then the cat would take on the role of reminding drivers of the speed limit, by sitting in the road. I held the most affection for High-vis-vest Man, whom I often saw walking down the middle of the road on his twice-daily walk from the retirement home. His wooden walking stick was so worn that the bottom fanned outwards like a circular broom. In time the stick became replaced by a zimmer frame, but I still had to swerve the bike to avoid colliding with him.

I passed the brown and white sign of a skier that indicated one was leaving Aude for the mountainous Ariège. Winter

202

was lingering in the crisp air, and as I rounded the crest of the hill to drop down into the Ariège, I saw that first glimpse of the jagged chain of the Pyrenees, the pyramids looming white against the sky and broken up by patches of grey haze that denoted the valleys. I always felt a thrill at that point. It wasn't just the frisson from spotting the familiar silhouette of the summits; there was also an emotion sparked by the indistinctness of the haze, knowing that somewhere within that nebulous grey was my Pyrenean home.

My mind wandered to what I knew about my new neighbours. The house next door, with its concrete stairs and leaking roof, had recently sold to a young couple. Vincent had told me a few snippets about them. Olivier was a local man who'd harboured a dream to live in the hamlet ever since he'd walked through it daily on the way to school. He was moving in with Marianne, and together they were hoping to convert the land into something that would sustain them. I felt slightly nervous when Vincent described Olivier as a hunter. *Was that his job?* I asked, envisioning a string of slaughtered animals pegged up outside my windows. Vincent snorted, reminding me that hunting wasn't an actual *career* in France.

I need not have worried. Staggering up the path with a week's worth of supplies, it was instantly clear that the place had been transformed with a more lived-in look, one that was undeniably untidy but nevertheless seemed to suit the ageing hamlet. My house at the end of the track now had the beginnings of a smallholding rising up around it, with rabbits to one side and *poussins* out the front that were plagued by a frolicking ginger kitten. The slope behind the house was dotted with the brown and white of sheep and their tottering lambs, with chickens fenced off to the side; whichever happened to be closest to the house could be heard loud and clear down the chimney, which was at the same height as the slope. A sheepdog puppy eyed me suspiciously as he wandered among the items lying in front of the houses: portable vegetable beds, a sheet of drying onions, old pots and pans, a lemon tree and even a cement mixer.

Marianne came out to apologise for the mess, acknowledging that it was *comme un bazar* but that they were still getting themselves straight. I honestly didn't mind. I could see that they had a mammoth job to get the house properly habitable, and at the same time they were trying to clear the slopes around to extend the grazing area. It was certainly cluttered and yes, it looked like an open-air junk store, yet somehow it all felt right, as if the land was being restored to its original purpose. The surrounding forest had been shaved, but with glints of sunlight now visible among the carpet of dried leaves, it all seemed less forbidding. Even the edges of the old terraces had been brought more clearly into relief as they were now bordered by piles of sliced logs interspersed with neatly stacked discarded branches.

We gradually got to know each other, *petit à petit* as they say. Trying out John's theory that incomers have a duty to show the French our food customs, I cautiously offered them the odd English treat, such as a couple of bottles of Devon craft beer that exploded in yeasty froth when they were opened. I handed Olivier a packet of Cornish clotted cream cookies that he ripped open and munched before I could explain the meaning of the words *Rugged Cornwall* on the packet. Marianne would painstakingly explain the different vegetables that she grew, introducing me to a creamy vegetable dish that I'd never heard of – *potiron marron* – and I tried unsuccessfully to copy. I bought vegetables from her and received the odd gift of presumably unsellable carrots that had great chunks nibbled away by some unidentified pest. They agreed to check an academic abstract that I'd written in French, poring over it together, eager to improve my clumsy attempt. I handed them a long-term loan of the key to my old garage that sat at the side of the track, knowing that it was more valuable to them with all of their stuff. In return Olivier cut down an overhanging tree that had threatened to flatten the flimsy structure, filling a corner of the garage with neat 50cm lengths to fit my fireplace.

Every now and then they'd make an effort to involve me in something that they thought I'd be interested in. Once I met them on the lane when they were moving the sheep and they handed me a silver-handled crook so I could keep up the rear. Another evening the dusky silence was punctuated by a strange bark, followed by a hammering on the door. I opened it to see Olivier standing in the dark with a deer suspended upside down from his left hand. 'Is it dead?' I asked. It was the deer who answered with the same bark I'd heard moments before, raising its head to gaze at me from the humiliation of being dangled with its feet tied together. They explained that they'd found it, sick, in the forest and had carried it back so that a vet could investigate. A discussion ensued as to exactly what kind of deer it was, with concern that they got the English name right. It turned out to be a roe deer. I left them to it and gently closed the door on the spectacle of Olivier stepping onto a set of weighing scales as Marianne passed him the strung-up deer.

Another evening they banged on the door, shouting, and I opened it, expecting to find some catastrophe, but instead I was pulled out to come and look at an unusually spectacular sunset. A deep red haze was suspended over the Massat valley, part of the *mer de nuages* that I'd seen drifting that way whilst out walking earlier. We wandered along the hillside to gain a better view of the phenomenon, watching the shape turn from red to gold along its edges. 'We're lucky – lucky? – to be here,' murmured Marianne, testing her English. I nodded. It wasn't an easy life, what with tending the sheep and the chickens, flitting between the different allotments to plant, tend and harvest everything, getting up early to do the markets and trying to renovate the big old house with its leaking roof. But it was a life they had chosen, just as the English incomers had chosen theirs, although the smallholding was a long way from Elaine's manicured lawn with chickens alongside.

Being local, Olivier had instilled the project with a sense of continuity in terms of place, and together they were slowly picking up the pieces of how people had lived here in an earlier age. Unexpectedly, their arrival also helped to deepen my own sense of familiarity and connection with the landscape. The previous owners had rarely ventured from the house during their short visits; Claude had spent his time on the renovations while Sandrine sat reading in the shade. I often told them where I'd been out walking, which was met with a polite interest, but the names of places and summits didn't appear to mean a great deal to them.

This profoundly changed with the arrival of Olivier and Marianne. Olivier in particular had an exceptionally detailed knowledge of the area, having spent years in these mountains. The first time he came inside, he walked around scrutinising the photographs I'd put on the walls, pretty much naming the exact spot where I'd stood to take each photo. He began suggesting various peaks, passes and routes for me, some of which turned out to be spectacular and to which I returned over and over. If he saw me exhaustedly walking up the path at the end of the day, he would want to know where I'd been, always nodding and explaining the route to Marianne, and usually dropping in the fact that he'd once run it in one hour and twenty minutes, compared to my five or six hours of plodding. Nevertheless, I learned to take care with understanding his instructions. When Terry and I walked into Spain, we followed a route that I thought he'd described as "flat", but he could only have been referring to the initial approach along the valley floor, as over the course of the day we climbed a height gain of 1,456m.

Of the hunting there was little evidence, apart from a jar of wild boar pâté that they brought round one evening. I even made friends with the scruffy sheepdog, which was a first for me, being a cat person. I got used to the dog following me around and coming to lie with his head on my feet when I sat outside. I didn't care about the dirt he transferred from his paws as he jumped up, although Marianne would always tell him to stop, crying *Michelle est propre!* – Michelle is clean! I grew used to hearing the late afternoon "clock" of the chainsaw starting up when Olivier came home from work, glancing out to see him balanced on the hillside, one hand on his hip, single-handedly shearing the forest. I learned to wait patiently on the track with my bike while chains from a tractor pulled yet another felled ash tree out of the way. I got used to falling asleep to the chime of bells when the sheep were pastured in my "back garden", and I even learned to blank out the Sunday 6am hammering as the couple panicked to patch up the DIY disaster they'd inherited. Juliette had been absolutely right when she'd said that whoever bought that house would need to begin all over again.

Epilogue

THE END OF THE TRACK?

===

Before this journey, I'd been curious about the English incomers living in this corner of France; what brought them here? How did they feel about being English among that stereotype of cliquey British expats with their half-baked dreams? Did they feel social pressure to be the right kind of incomer, and not like the dreaded "others"?

I'd learned that it was too easy to be critical of the other English, and if people's behaviour flew a bit close to the stereotype – and it often did – then they just manipulated their way around any sense of hypocrisy. *We have a duty to show the French what we eat; it's the fault of the French for not understanding our pronunciation; it's easier to use the internet than ask the locals; we aren't the kind of people to socialise,* and so forth. It would have been easy to ridicule it all, just like the trolls on the forum; instead, I began to see it as understandable. If the way the incomers behaved was often contradictory to the attitudes and the values that they espoused, it was their way of maintaining a sense of self in a world full of irony.

That Mirepoix menu, which I'd shown people as an afterthought, turned out to reflect the contradictions perfectly.

Almost everyone decried the café – *it's not what I'm here for* – but almost universally they went on to talk about when they'd visited it. Faced with an interviewer, it was tempting to show disdain and question why anyone would want to eat bread pudding in France. Yet should a move to another country mean a total refusal to indulge in something you'd previously enjoyed?

Some of the incomers worried about being seen to inflict their English culture, as if they were colonials imposing their way of life on the locals. Perhaps this wasn't really surprising when journalists talked about a British invasion; admittedly it was tongue-in-cheek, and from what I'd seen, the British incomers who'd made their way to Ariège were a sparse and unthreatening lot. But there was a clear reluctance to be seen as not imposing an English culture, or being insensitive to local customs. In Pat's words, 'I bought a box of crackers for them 'cause they've never seen them before and I said it's a *tradition anglais* and they just loved that I'd thought about it. That isn't imposing on them, but just showing them a little different quirk that we have.'

During the course of my research, I'd often been asked how the French perceived the English incomers. It was impossible to generalise from anecdotal evidence; looking back over my notes, I'd noticed that three individuals had mentioned that they had sensed a chilly response at the post office, although that could have been down to one cashier. On the whole, people talked as if they felt they'd been accepted; not exactly with wild French enthusiasm for their English neighbours, but acceptance and tolerance. Pat and John's perception of being treated like royalty was the exception, although Lynn talked about having to hide from the garrulous locals who wanted to talk to her and who had been nothing but kind. It perhaps helped that she lived in one of the valleys that had been at the heart of bear training, where almost every family had either a member living in the United States or one who had returned. Certainly Juliette had looked bemused when I raised the question of possible French resentment against English incomers. 'Everyone is welcome here,' she said, shaking her head.

Something else that surprised me was the dissatisfaction that almost everyone claimed to feel at their level of French, especially those who'd spent years learning and came to feel that being "good" was never going to be enough. This was down to how people saw themselves in relation to what they'd imagined before the move – the ideal self. Academics call this kind of need or motivation *integrative,* as it relates to an emotional and social need to fit in. Susan and Gerald seemed to be motivated primarily by this need to be socially competent and to lessen the cultural gap.

Those who needed to work also had an *instrumental* motivation; a more practical necessity to learn a language. You could argue that this was a basic aspect of living in France for everyone; nevertheless, some people tried to manage without it, although it was difficult for those who needed to work. For Lynn, Tina and Emma, their ability was reasonable but not quite enough to be comfortable in the kind of employment they'd been used to. While they also talked about emotional needs, where "it's just not the same" to socialise with French people, the instrumental factors, the practical issues, might also lead people to pack up and return to the UK.

For Pat and John, learning on a need-to-know basis was good enough. They'd made an effort; they appeared to manage on the whole and had probably reached their expected level. Whenever I set foot in a French DIY store I'd hear, in my head, John's Midland vowels slowly repeating the mantra: *That's what they call a saw, that's what they call a lawnmower.*

210

For them, being invited and welcomed to social gatherings was more important than being fluent, even if their pronunciation of *pain au raisins* was incomprehensible to others. Thrilled with their reception by the French, they took delight in being treated as something different, *the English*.

In contrast, the conversation with Emma and Mitch oozed tensions between the ideal integrated French-speaking incomer, and what turned out to be their reality. But such tensions were smoothed out by an insistence that they hadn't imagined anything different, and what's more, in every other way they did things right – not like the part-timers. To sum it up, it was all presented in black and white terms, a kind of binary system where you were either the right or the wrong kind of British incomer.

A PLACE OF TRANSIENCE

As time went on it became clear that the Ariège was a transient place for many. It wasn't just the young Ariégeois who left; fast-forward a few years and not many of the incomers I'd met were still living there.

On that late summer morning in Gerald's courtyard, I'd detected an air that something was missing. Along with his acknowledgement that Sandra would really rather be closer to family, it all foreshadowed a likely future back in England. In the event it took three years. There was no doubt that they were happy with how their six years of small town Ariège life had turned out, but they were needed elsewhere.

The brilliant family, aware that they had passed that crucial third Ariège winter, had nevertheless already sold up and moved out by the following summer. Valley Cottage, so painstakingly built and movingly named by Lynn and

Steve, was on the market before it was even finished, its walls enveloping a sense of relief that they would one day return to family and the English culture they professed to miss.

I'd often cycled past Elaine's "English" house and noted that the shutters were closed; according to Susan, the pair were often back in England, visiting family. Trying to track down Tina, I discovered that the shop she'd worked in had shut down a few years after our chat and that she'd moved away. Even Felicity, the most settled old-timer, had decided to retire early, and rather than remain in Ariège as planned, they'd uprooted out of the département to somewhere further east. Less surprising was the speed at which Dylan had abandoned the collapsed yurt, leaving the barn to continue its passage into decay, no doubt to the glee of the resident *loirs*.

So there were many practical reasons why people left, mostly connected with the need to work and stay close to family back in England. Yet there was something else that nagged at me. The whole idea of "moving to France for a better life" was a generic phenomenon that sometimes blurred the distinctiveness of place. To some incomers, Ariège could have been anywhere in France, as long as it had the right house. The country itself was sometimes an amorphous backdrop, affordable "France", a commodity that people didn't always examine beyond its ability to offer the right house at the right price. It seemed too easy to come to the Ariège inhabiting an idea rather than a place, and when the idea became the place, it was not always what people had imagined or intended.

It therefore wasn't surprising that some people became disenchanted and moved on, especially if they'd drifted into the Ariège because they couldn't afford where they really wanted to be. They'd come to France for a better life, and if something wasn't right, then it might finally dawn on them that it was the wrong village, region or even country for what they'd been looking for.

I'd read a few posts on the forum from members saying their goodbyes as they prepared to move elsewhere in France or over the border to Spain. They talked about going in search of more settled weather and less rain, more opportunities to indulge in social and cultural events and more tourists to occupy their gîtes.

A more reliable presence was that of the Mirepoix café. One rainy and deserted Sunday I had time to kill in Mirepoix and walked past it, noting that it had changed owners yet again and the chalkboard menu was now all in French – *gateau de carotte* replacing the *carotte cake*. The door opened into a steamy atmosphere and the sounds of Midlands accents. Just one other table was occupied and I sat beneath a string of stuffed fabric hearts hanging above my head, embroidered with fluffy slogans such as *There's no place like home*. The walls were dotted with various English menus advertising cream teas, toasted teacakes and the like. I could see a few dozen English paperback titles stacked up on a tall bookshelf, with a notice advertising English book exchanges, here and at Léran, to support a cancer charity. The male owner shouted my order in English to the young French chef.

The couple sitting there were happy to strike up a conversation, describing their holiday home nearby that they'd found on the internet. Like so many of the others they'd originally wanted something further east. They made their house sound rather grand, describing how it had previously been renovated and extended by an English banker and his team of British builders. They asked me where I was from. 'How do you manage with the cold up in the mountains?' asked Dave. I shrugged my shoulders. 'I just dress in layers, and saw some wood when I really need to warm up.'

'We've brought a log burner over with us, in the car, but it's just sitting there. We can't seem to find out how to get it installed,' he said.

Mary nodded. 'Can't find anyone to do it.' The language barrier had possibly been a factor there, although they glossed over it.

'We manage to get by,' smiled Dave.

'And everyone's really helpful,' chipped in Mary. They had been deep in conversation with the owner when I arrived, enjoying a bit of familiar English comfort on the Sunday when winter had finally arrived.

A few months later, on yet another dismal Sunday at the end of a winter that had lingered for far too long, I opened the door of the café to find it was devoid of customers. Ordering from the cake display, I tried not to eavesdrop on the conversation between the French chef and the owner who spoke slowly back at him in English. The conversation ended when a young man came in and sat down to play chess with the chef. The owner drew up his chair to talk to me. I was curious about how viable it was to stay open on Sundays throughout the winter, and he assured me that it was – there were sufficient visits from the English incomers, as well as the French, to make it worthwhile. The phone rang and he disappeared. I pulled a book from the bookcase, left a few euros as donation in the charity box, and left the warmth of the café to pick my way over the icy cobbles back to the car.

Finally, what about my own journey as I'd travelled around the Ariège talking to the English – had I deepened an understanding of my own place here? People had enjoyed talking about their experiences but occasionally I'd caught a glimpse of myself through their eyes. For some I was a fellow Brit in France with whom they would happily meet again over dinner; others had slotted me into the category of the irritating "part-timers". For Dylan and his entourage I was the owner of a "proper house", someone who automatically binned food that dropped onto the floor, and who used the normal supermarket entrance rather than dipping into the skips around the back.

Despite the tendency to place people into binary categories, in reality we were all part of a dynamic, shifting mosaic of incomers. I felt the strings of a loose connection with everyone, yet not through any bind of nationality. It was more an association through place. Juliette got closest to it when she tried to make sense of our connections, saying that we were all there at the end of that track because we "love nature". No matter our original reasons for arriving in the Ariège, those of us who stayed did so because of how we felt when we gazed out on that corner of the Pyrenees.

NOT A BARGAINING CHIP

Fast-forward again to the summer of 2016 and the shock result of the Brexit referendum. At the time of writing, Britons face an uncertain future regarding their right to reside in France. Much of this uncertainty hangs on the question of guaranteed residency rights of EU nationals living in Britain that would mirror reciprocal rights for Britons living in other EU countries.

While the press has often focused on the uncertainty of EU migrants within the UK, there are many Brits in Europe who feel themselves to be in limbo and ignored. And even when the media gives them attention, articles are often supported with stereotypical images of Brits sitting around in Spanish bars draped with Union flags, portraying a kind of cheaper and sunnier Little England. All of this conveys the idea of people with sufficient privilege to escape the UK greyness, "ex-pats" who spend their time sitting around drinking together. Why would the so-called "left-behind" who voted out care about what happens to these advantaged few? Yet the largest numbers of Brits in Europe are of working age, forming a significant British element in the EU labour market.[30] Another interesting figure to emerge is the estimated number of British citizens in France, given as 157,062, in second place behind Spain. This is not a particularly high number, especially considering that the number of French citizens living in the UK is actually higher. It all helps to balance the earlier media articles that talked about the waves of Brits "flooding" into France, the "British invasion" of property seekers.

Some fifteen months after the Brexit referendum I managed to catch up with Susan. It was one of those late summer days when the Ariège rain clouds refuse to budge and I'd spent the morning killing time by dodging puddles in Saint-Girons, and pondering on the permanent closure of so many shops, including Lidl. Now, sitting damply in a café, I could sense that her fury hadn't weakened at all over the year. 'I'm as angry now as I was back then,' she grimaced. 'I don't feel comfortable with being English and I certainly don't trust the UK government to sort it out properly. And I really resent being seen as a bargaining chip.' She confessed that she was pursuing the opportunity to take Irish citizenship in order to retain an EU foothold, but this wasn't an option open to her partner, so it was only a partial solution. 'I do feel a link with the Irish,' she said, 'and I've always felt European. I thought that would be enough, and it would be there forever. We've considered going off to live in other countries at some point, but now we feel really restricted.' What did she mean by that? 'We're afraid to move from France in case we lose our residency status,' she explained. 'And I really worry that the other EU states will get so annoyed with the UK that they'll make it difficult in reciprocation. If the UK's not being reasonable, then why should they be?' she questioned.

---

30   Fewer Britons living in EU than previously thought, study finds. *The Guardian*, 27 January 2017.

She had other significant worries, including financial anxiety that revolved around the fluctuating exchange rate, which had diminished their pensions dramatically. In addition, no one knew what would happen to the basic free healthcare provision that they received in France. 'We pay the top-up mutual but what's going to happen to our entitlement to the basic?' she asked.

I asked her if she felt that the issue of Britons in the EU had seemed neglected, with the focus more on EU citizens in the UK. 'Well, yes,' she said, 'but I feel *desperately* sorry for them. Those working families, with children in schools, houses bought, I feel so angry on their behalf too, not just my own. Their situation is far worse. What happens to families with children born in different countries?'

I was beginning to sense a disconnection with Britain. She furrowed her eyebrows, trying to find a better word to sum up her feelings. 'It's a dislocation,' she said. 'The link is broken. The world has got smaller, but at the same time we've become further removed from England.' I knew that six years ago she'd professed to be totally uninterested in the idea of a return to England, and I guessed that this hadn't changed. 'Absolutely no, not England,' she said. 'I might consider Scotland though,' she mused, 'but not England, *not ever.*'

I left Susan with the gloom of Brexit making the day feel even greyer and damper than before. As I drove home, a thought began to grow. Six years ago, when travelling around talking with the English incomers, I'd been overwhelmed by their efforts not to be seen as part of a British network. They mostly knew each other but were at pains to play it down. And while they depended on each other for advice on the forum, that very same site had included warnings about such dependence. Yet now there was a much more serious threat in the form of Brexit, and I wondered whether this would lead to the Brits in France forgetting their irritations with each other. Who cared now about the morals of eating bacon and bread pudding when your right to continue living in France was on shaky ground?

The more I thought about it, the more I anticipated a sea change in how prepared people were to identify as part of a British network. People had always sought out the expatriate network, whether they admitted it or not, both as a practical solution but also due to an emotional need to retain a link with who or what was familiar to them; what one forum member termed "the comfort of expats". That emotional need was still there, but it was heightened now, as everyone found themselves within a common situation of uncertainty. This would surely generate a need for a more practical solidarity, strength in numbers. And the tangible signs were there, with people joining networks such as the buoyant RIFT (Remain in France Together) network, a campaigning and support group with thousands of members that described itself as *Working together to protect the rights of UK citizens living in France.*

So after all that avoidance of being seen as part of the *Brits in France* phenomenon, and the efforts to draw a boundary between oneself and everyone else, there were signs at last of a stronger manifestation of a British-in-France identity. It had always been there, of course, a sometimes uncomfortable reminder of who the incomers were. Now it was becoming more tangible, something to welcome against the common threat.

ACKNOWLEDGEMENTS

This book was made possible by the willingness of the English incomers to welcome me into their lives and talk through their experiences over endless cups of tea. I give heartfelt thanks to them all. Names and identifying details have been changed to maintain privacy.

I would also like to thank my family for their encouragement during the writing of this book. Thanks are due too to members of the Department of Linguistics and English Language at Lancaster University, for giving advice and guidance during the original academic study.

If you have enjoyed this book, please consider leaving a review on Amazon or Goodreads. You can find more writing and evocative images from Ariège and other places at www.michelle-lawson.com.

CPSIA information can be obtained
at www.ICGtesting.com
Printed in the USA
BVHW041752260120
570542BV00014B/284